PRAISE FOR JAY FALCO
TRACK TO PROS

"The real power of Jay Falcone's Fast Track to Prosperity is that the advice it offers those looking to take control of their personal finances is both relatable and usable. Falcone helps clear the path to financial literacy and motivates us to complete the journey because, as he asks, "If **you** don't care about your personal finances, who will?""

—L. Elliott Pierre
MAC City Show Host and Owner of Greenlight Creative

"Fast Track to Prosperity is an excellent guide that includes clear, actionable steps to help you transform your financial future for the better. There's something for everybody in Fast Track to Prosperity, no matter where you're starting your financial journey from today. Author Jay Falcone has refined the content in this book through hundreds of hours working with real Canadians from diverse backgrounds. That experience gels together perfectly within these book covers."

—Jay Seabrook
COO and Co-founder of Enriched Academy

"Financial Literacy is the basis of a solid, well-rounded education. Fast Track to Prosperity provides you with the tools to increase your financial knowledge and manage your money responsibly."

—Bertha Fairley
Dean, School of Continuing Education – Keyano College

"Falcone has honed his message into clear, digestible, and practical information accessible to anyone interested in taking power over their own financial future. This is the perfect book for those beginning to learn about personal finance, or for anyone looking for a refresher."

—Therese Greenwood
Executive Director - Multicultural Association of Wood Buffalo

RESULTS from Past Participants of the Financial Literacy Program (FLP)

"I consider myself fortunate to have completed the financial literacy course taught by Jay Falcone. He challenged our creativity and curiosity in the world of financial concepts and practices.

As an entrepreneur, some of the key learnings that helped me better manage my business were understanding the concept of realized and unrealized gains and losses and how to calculate net worth.

I also learned about which stage of my business to change the structure from a personal small business to a corporation to maximize growth and reduce taxes."

—Ramazan Nassery
Immigration Consultant

"Ever since I attended the first class on Budgets, I was able to start budgeting and keep track of my net cash flow from my accounts. The simple process I learned has helped me see where my largest expenses were and better control my finances. Having more net income at the end of every month means I have funds to invest.

The course covers a lot of material that is basic but that I needed to hear again. More importantly, it's also challenged me to think differently about my finances."

—Nag Babu
Engineer

"As new immigrants to this country, my wife and I were very fortunate to attend the Financial Literacy Program with Jay Falcone.

We have learned a lot since then. We managed to improve our credit score and paid off most of our significant debt.

To this date, we still ask Jay for advice on financial matters and "the way of life" here in Canada. Thank you very much, our friend."

—Jennifer and Renie Dela Paz
Security Guard and Chef

"The Financial Literacy Program (FLP) helped me understand the Canadian financial basics. I also learnt a lot about different investment strategies and how to evaluate a company's stock. With this knowledge, I have built up significant investments in the stock market."

—Csaba Horvath
Leader, Field Services Technician

"From the Financial Literacy Program, I was successfully able to increase my knowledge on investments. I started investing after the course and realized a newfound confidence in my choices. Furthermore, as a beginner, I was able to acquire 23-28% profit over a span of two years."

—Minal Trivedi
Accounting Associate

"As a result of taking Jay's Financial Program, I've learned how to budget and better control my finances. I've also acquired an appreciation of stocks and general investments. Every bit of the course has helped me better understand money and finances. I am so grateful to Jay for giving me this opportunity."

—Laju Kapasi
Freelance Media Advisor

"Taking the course, I finally grasped the consequences of our "Debt Trap". Through the examples and strategies I learned, I was able to better understand my financial situation, appropriately plan, track and come out of our debt as planned.

This gave me the freedom to start pursuing other financial goals. I now have the basics to start investing in the stock market and ideas for alternate sources of income."

—Angela Nino and Mauricio Beltran
Practical Nurse and Mechanical Engineer

"Since taking the FLP, I was able to develop my short- and long-term goals and I have more confidence in my financial plan. These are some of my other learnings:

I have a better understanding of taxes that will help me save money in the long run. I know how to get my credit report and ways to improve my score. I have some ideas on starting my own business. Finally, I've learned how to read financial statements and more comfortable investing."

Wilfredo Temundo
Operations Director, MacDonald's

"Financial literacy wasn't taught in school where I attended. Coming to Canada as an immigrant wasn't easy and attending the Financial Literary Program has helped me "big time" in dealing with my finances and the goals that I have set for myself and my family. Since starting the course, I have developed my short- and long-term goals and review them frequently with my husband.

Jay is an excellent instructor, and I am grateful to him and the courses he taught us. He's helped us become more financially literate and developed a better wealth mindset as well. His works need be shared with all worldwide so that people can be more prosperous in life and in turn build better communities."

—Ann Morehouse
Client Advisor and Online Business Owner/Entrepreneur

"Since taking the course, I have a better understanding of general business and financial concepts. I now feel confident enough to move from lower to medium-risk investments and thereby better diversifying my portfolio.

In addition, the Program definitely helped me organize my financial habits and establish a routine of watching the business news with a renewed interest and understanding."

—Carole Cameron
Airline Pilot

"After enrolling in the Financial Literacy Program facilitated by Jay, I was really impressed and positively impacted by the training. The courses were very detailed, and the lessons were delivered in a simple and easy to understand manner. Before I took the program, I used to buy stocks based on recommendations from self-acclaimed "stock market gurus" without doing proper research and I have gotten my fingers burnt severely.

After going through the course on Investments with Jay, I now know how to do due research and analyze companies before buying their stock. This new knowledge has boosted my confidence in self-directed investing, and I am even able to teach others what I have learnt!"

—Adeola Monofi

Financial Advisor and Director of Klan Luxury Inc.

"After my wife and I attended Jay's Financial Literacy Program, we were able to set clear goals and periodically review them to ensure we were on track.

One of our goals was to purchase a rental property with a 50% down payment. We realized that goal by taking possession on September, 2021. We have also diversified our investment portfolio from Bitcoin and other cryptocurrencies to different stocks."

—Alejandro Otalora

Systems Engineer

"I enrolled in the Program after hearing about it in my English for new Canadians class. Since taking the Financial sessions, I've learned about budgets and developing more reasonable spending habits.

The class on tax-advantaged investments was very interesting and eye-opening and as a result, I have opened an RRSP (Registered Retirement Savings Plan)."

—**Agata Czeslawa Stosz**
Office Admin Assistant

"The course was certainly very useful as I learned a lot about Canadian banking, income tax, the importance of making financial plans, taking care of my credit, investments, saving for retirement, Government Sponsored programs, insurance and of course, awareness of identify fraud. I am very grateful that you took the time to share your knowledge with us. Since taking the course, I have:

- started budgeting and I'm able to save $1,000 a month :)
- a better understanding of income taxes
- developed a habit of reading and researching about investments
- been able to increase my credit score
- a better understanding of insurance"

—**Lyanna Borges Furtado**
Heavy Equipment Operator

"I am so thankful I signed up for Jay Falcone's Level 2 Financial literacy course. I gained knowledge about investments and using the information from the course, I have changed how I invest and have already realized a 5% return rate on my new investments in the last 8-month period. Jay has a budget worksheet that is clear, user-friendly, and easy to understand. Working through our personal budget with Jay, I was able to recognize where I could save money while living comfortably today. Even more exciting, he helped me figure out our retirement time frame and level of income we would require in our golden years."

—Sandy Grandison
Administrator

"I was a participant in Jay's Financial Literacy Program, and I can say that it really changed the way I deal with my finances. I started investing in stocks and learned the importance of reading annual reports, analyzing financial ratios to determine where the company is headed and if a stock is valuable and has potential for growth. My gain from stock investments has significantly grown and I will be continuing with my research and invest more. Your future is in your hands and the first step you can take is to take the course and learn valuable lessons on how you can prosper financially."

—Milena Parviz
HR Professional

"After attending the course, I revisited my stock portfolio and learned more about how to properly choose these investments. I also learned how to write out my short-term and long-term term goals and how to keep them in check so I could achieve them."

—Abegail Cunan
Project Controls Advisor, OJ Pipelines

"Attending the sessions helped me a lot with my financial goals and plans in life. It taught me the importance of revisiting my goals and plans by carefully fine-tuning them.

I really enjoyed the weekly assignments where we had to read business news and summarize what we learned. By the end of the program, my understanding of financially-related news definitely increased."

—Joan Guerrero
Administrator, MacDonalds

"Jay explains each topic in the course clearly and I've been able to significantly increase my financial literacy. Now when I read or watch the business news, I can relate and understand it a lot better. With Jay's help, I've learned a lot about Canadian banking, income tax, the importance of making financial plans, taking care of my credit, investments, saving for retirement, insurance and fraud.

The best part is that Jay inspired and encouraged us to keep on learning and to apply all the learnings in our everyday life. I am truly grateful to our mentor Jay Falcone for inspiring us and educating us."

—John Bernardo

Restaurant Maintenance, Photographer

"I am happy that I was able to attend the Financial Literacy seminar, taught by Jay Falcone. Moving to a new country is hard enough, having a guide to navigate the system is priceless. Jay showed the way to become comfortable with taxes, saving and investing. He made an otherwise "dry" material fun by sharing stories and anecdotes to emphasize the concepts being taught. We are all affected by money, so why not learn to manage what we have."

—Uylander Jack

Educator, Intentional Immigrants Channel
- YouTube and Podcast.
www.intentionalimmigrants.com

"Given the abundance of information, the ability to cut through the noise in order to provide busy adult-students with filtered information in a comprehensive format that takes into account their diverse perspectives and financial knowledge is a big determining factor in the success of a financial literacy course.

Jay Falcone has designed his financial literacy course to not only provide the necessary information, but also to deliver accumulated knowledge from his professional experience in an engaging and interactive way. The class also served as a gathering place for people who share similar interests, resulting in a significant course bounce!"

—Hichem Aiedi
Entrepreneur

"As a result of taking the course, I have better understanding of the real estate market and I have started working towards owning my first rental property.

I have also gained a deeper insight on multiple sources of income and looking forward to expanding my home-based business beyond its current state. Finally, what I enjoyed the most about the Program was Jay's accessibility and dedication and the ability to review the recorded lessons at my leisure."

—Ike Dada
Banking Advisor, RBC (Royal Bank of Canada)

"My journey into personal finances started with the financial literacy program presented by Jay Falcone. The program helped me to acknowledge and structure my financial goals both in short and long term.

I was able to learn financial principles and how I could implement it to my day-to-day life. Moreover, the program helped me to seek investment opportunities, and to create multiple streams of income in a short period of time. Thank you, Jay."

—Nardos Weldemariam
Occupation- Registered Nurse

"Through the Financial Literacy Program, as a new immigrant, I was able to understand the banking system and financial resources available.

I was also able to start developing a wealth mindset by controlling spending, living on a budget, and managing personal finances. This was a major step in starting to live without debt and possessing the financial ability to take on new investment opportunities."

—Mario Kieffer
Civil Designer

"Through the course, I was able to grow my financial knowledge and confidence in managing my money, paying my bills, borrowing and responsibly saving money and how and why to invest and plan for retirement.

I now have the skills to interpret financial documents and topics, and actually understand what they mean.

I started a budget, and this helped me to save every month; protect my savings for any emergency and increase investments. It has also assisted me in my business in managing expenses and saving money.

I am very happy that the financial literacy knowledge has helped me to secure and ensure an income for retirement."

—**Nandini Mehta**
Postal Worker

"The Program shifted my paradigm on how I view finances. Throughout the program, my eyes were opened to the different types of opportunities to make money and create multiple income streams for financial freedom.

I am now actively investing in many assets such as stocks, index funds, NFTs, foreign exchange and cryptocurrency. I can proudly say that Jay Falcone's class has impacted me greatly and made me into the person I am today."

—**Noah Dalupang**
Investor

"Even though I had a basic understanding of finances, with Jay's help, I was able to lay down a foundation for taking my finances more seriously. I can say with certainty this was one of my best decisions.

Your task on goal setting was instrumental in my learning how to set financial goals. This exercise has also subsequently helped me in my professional career with holding myself accountable financially. I had never set one goal in my life until your course.

Since taking the program, I have zero debt apart from my Mortgage in which I have set a goal to also pay off, invested well in stocks and have done very well, have made a budget in which I track and stay on top of weekly, track my net worth monthly, read more books and currently work with a well-educated financial coach."

—Simon McKean
Maintenance Supervisor

"Since taking this course, I've started my own home business as another stream of income and also taken advantage of all the tax benefits! The course was a real eye-opener!"

—Rick Ryan
Business Owner

"In taking the course, I learned many lessons such as credit, insurance and income tax that would be such a critical part of

the road to becoming an independent adult!!

Going to school, I wasn't sure if I was ever going to use linear algebra very often, but I knew I would need to start paying for my own insurance and start saving money for my future!

One of the best lessons that I am glad I was able to start early was the importance of budgeting and establishing goals. I now have a 1, 5 and 10 year. I review them often and because my mom made the decision to enroll me in Jay's course, I am confident I have the tools to achieve my goals!"

—Cassidy Star Sneddon
University Student

"Before taking the course, I hadn't really thought about my Core Values in terms of finances. Since that first lesson in class, I've been basing my decisions on my Core Values, which have really helped me in the financial aspect of my life."

—Angelica D Borja
Student

"Thank you for giving me the opportunity to participate in the Financial Literacy program. I was able to gain a lot of knowledge and it provided me the tools to better manage money and debt. The program helped me obtain an overall sense of financial wellbeing and self-confidence. As a result of attending the Program, I've started budgeting and saving $350 per month. My daughter and I began investing in the stock market for the first time. I've applied some of the cost-saving ideas from tax lesson in my business. Thank you so much giving us great knowledge."

—Suraksha Patel
Educational Assistant

"Since taking Jay's courses, I've opened a new bank account with services that meet both my needs and goals. I have a better understanding of how our Canadian progressive tax system works and how to make it work for me. I opened a cryptocurrency account. I feel more confident in choosing both public and private stocks. I plan to start an ETF account. I have a newfound confidence in Real Estate and am planning to purchase a second property. These courses are full of "golden nuggets" and my financial knowledge has increased significantly."

—Stacey Park
Transit Bus Dispatcher/Scheduler

"As a newcomer to this country, adapting to different financial responsibilities was a struggle. After taking Jay Falcone's Financial Literacy course, I have a better understanding of the importance of good credit and financial literacy.

Important decisions such as purchasing a new vehicle, renting a new space, and even buying a home is a lot to take in. It even shocked my husband who has lived here longer and owns his own business.

The course offers a lot of basic information that people claim to know but it is good to hear again. My husband even used the information from the course and implemented it in his business."

—Journey and Marcin Biel
Site Employee and Business Owner

"Mr. Falcone was very generous in teaching us financial literacy. Many of the students in the class were new to Canada and Mr. Falcone was kind enough to share his knowledge on how Canadian banking works, how to best utilize a credit card, how to set up RESP (Registered Education Savings Plans) accounts, among many other things.

I could see how thankful and appreciative every student was. Mr. Falcone answered questions thoroughly and, in a manner, to ensure that everyone understood the concepts."

—Mia El Jamal
University Student

"Over the last several months, we took some positive actions from what we learned in the Program. We've opened a home-based business, made a successful plan to pay off our RV (Recreation vehicle) and put it in motion, and we are currently seeking a real estate investment opportunity I enjoyed the topics and found them relevant. The assignments were also helpful to reinforce the concepts learned."

—Tanya Ryan
Human Resources Professional

"Attending Jay Falcone's financial literacy classes changed my life for the better! I attended his course while I was a first-year university student and he helped me develop the financial literacy skills I needed to prepare me for adulthood.

These courses gave me the foundational skills and knowledge I needed to start my first business "Pumpkin & Finn" at 22 years of age.

Thanks to his teachings, I am able to manage both my personal and business finances with confidence."

—Naya Maria El Jamal
Small Business Owner, Pumpkin & Finn

Additional Praise About Jay Falcone and the Financial Literacy Program (FLP)

"In my time working with the Multicultural Association of Wood Buffalo (MCAWB), I saw firsthand the tremendous impact that the Financial Literacy Program (FLP) had on immigrant and refugee families.

The program provided participants with important information to support financial wellbeing, healthy financial habits, and future planning. I witnessed many families not only increase their knowledge and skills about the Canadian financial system but also improve their confidence and become empowered to make informed financial decisions for themselves and their families.

Financial literacy is a crucial step in successful integration and this program continues to support newcomers on that path."

—Caitlin Downie

MCAWB Program Manager (2013-2015), PhD Candidate

"As Program Manager, I had the privilege of observing Jay teach many sessions of the Financial Literacy Program. I was always impressed with how well he was able to engage students using real-time examples. I remember the 2017 cohort eagerly tracking Bitcoin each class on the whiteboard as it rose upwards of $25,000 CAN. Students were excited to learn and often shared how they were able to apply knowledge from the Financial Literacy Program to their everyday life, from understanding the basics of budgeting to buying their first investment home or developing an app as a second (or third) stream of income. Jay's classes had and continue to have a lasting impact on everyone that has taken part, MCA staff included."

—Jamie Desautels
MCAWB Program Manager (2016-2018), Policy Analyst for Public Health Agency of Canada

"Mr. Falcone was very generous with the knowledge that he shared in our Financial Literary course at the MCAWB. He was excellent at introducing newcomers to Canada to new financial concepts that they had never encountered before, and was very adept at adapting his instruction to his students' individual learning styles, using accessible language that they would understand."

Luay Eljamal,
MCAWB Programs & Communications Manager (2019-2020), Programs Manager of Arts Council Wood Buffalo

"There are a multitude of global studies and surveys that indicate a large gap in financial literacy within the population. Being financially literate enables an individual to be better prepared for those financial roadblocks, which, in turn, decreases the chances of personal economic distress.

Understanding this, Jay Falcone designed a comprehensive and practical Financial Literacy program for the community. Through Multicultural Association of Wood Buffalo, we are able to offer this important information to the public.

Jay facilitates this program in an easy-to-understand language which helps participants reach their financial goals.

He is thoughtful, methodical, empathetic, and personable. Jay's ability to explain complex concepts in clear language, combined with his empathetic nature and sound knowledge of money management consistently proves successful for participants. He helps individuals with the tools to develop a financial plan that is both realistic and satisfying."

—**Anurag Mathur**
MCAWB Programs &
Communications Manager (2020- 2022)

"Jay Falcone is a dedicated champion of financial literacy who has generously donated his time to helping others learn where their money goes.

The courses he has developed helps participants understand personal assets and liabilities and how to master spending by setting goals and budgeting. Then it is on to saving, investing, insurance, mortgages, the stock market and even cryptocurrency, all part of an easy-to-understand overview of the financial choices faced by everyone.

Falcone has honed his message into clear, digestible, and practical information accessible to anyone interested in taking power over their own financial future.

This is the perfect book for those beginning to learn about personal finance, or for anyone looking for a refresher."

—Therese Greenwood
Former MCAWB Executive Director of the Multicultural Association of Wood Buffalo and Author

FAST TRACK TO PROSPERITY

YOUR GUIDE TO FINANCIAL INDEPENDENCE

JAY FALCONE

First Edition 2022

ISBN: (epub) 978-1-949696-44-8
ISBN: (paperback) 978-1-949696-45-5

Printed in the United States of America
Published by:
Lasting Press
615 NW 2nd Ave #915
Canby, OR 97013

Cover and Interior Design by Rory Carruthers Marketing

Book Launch by Rory Carruthers Marketing

www.RoryCarruthers.com

For more information about **Jay Falcone** or to book him/her for your next event, speaking engagement, podcast, or media interview, please visit:
www.fasttrack2prosperity.com

To my loving parents, who instilled in me the value of hard work and persistence in every aspect of my life.

And in memory of my loving uncle (Zio) Antonio (Tony) Falcone, who himself was a gifted educator, avid reader and consummate storyteller. Although he was not here in person, his presence was felt throughout the book writing process.

CONTENTS

AN OPEN LETTER TO READERS

You're probably wondering, "Do we really need another book on personal finances?" Bookstore shelves and online offerings are littered with thousands of titles covering every aspect of managing your money. I know! I've done my share of reading them! But, while there are some excellent ones out there, a majority of them are as entertaining as going to an elaborate 50-course restaurant buffet and then choosing toast. Most books and online resources may attempt to teach an important financial concept. Still, the amount of detail and complexity of just one subject matter is daunting enough, let alone reading dozens to acquire a good, well-balanced knowledge of personal finance.

So, what makes this writing any different, you may ask? Well, before I give you my perspective as to why you should read it, I believe it's just as important for me to relay to you what this book is NOT. That way, you can decide upfront whether it's worth your money and, more importantly, your time, which is much more valuable.

This Book is NOT About a New Revelation or Concept

As I said above, I've read a lot of books over the years, so my financial knowledge comes from those writings and personal experiences. Most of what you will read in *Fast Track to Prosperity* has either been written or said by someone else. All

I've done is bundled some of that financial wisdom into a simple, achievable process and that have been used by hundreds of students to attain positive results.

I know I've come across the same financial concepts in various books, yet it wasn't about having the knowledge at that point. It was more about just doing it. In some cases, I had to hear the financial information several times, and by different authors, before finally kicking it into action. At times, that's the way it works for us.

This Book is NOT About Shaming you for Past and Poor Financial Decisions

In my introduction, you will quickly find out that I have made some unwise financial decisions in my life, just like anyone else. I come to you not as a financial genius but as someone who has experienced both wins and losses in the financial realm. As such, this book will NOT shame you about your financial past. In fact, it is so important to get your financial wellbeing and mindset in a proper space that I devote a whole chapter to it. I want to move you from Money Shame to Money Hope.

This Book is NOT Complex or Complicated

I know many folks like theories and in-depth guides on everything from budgeting to investing. There's nothing wrong with that, but you will not find it here. When I developed the Financial Literacy Program (FLP) for newcomers to Canada, I was keen on making it easy to understand. This way, individuals who may not have been exposed to financial systems and concepts (and in some cases even basic English), could easily attain this knowledge. The teaching had to be straightforward and practical, and the process revealed in *Fast Track to Prosperity* follows that premise. The dozens of success stories by participants in the FLP (some of which are documented in the book) testify that the most profound and life-changing truths are SIMPLE.

This Book is NOT About Formulas, Difficult Math and Statistics

Even though I use some statistics to drive home a point and get you to perform some basic math in calculating your net worth and a spending plan, there are no complex formulas or math in this reading. After all, numbers, averages and statistics may change, but the concepts do not. Understanding the complex details of how household debt is calculated for some government survey is useless to anyone if they don't take control of their own actual household debt first.

That's why I try to teach concepts rather than mathematical formulas. At the end of the day, it's not a question of financial knowledge; it's about taking action. This is the biggest challenge for many.

This Book is NOT Written for a Particular Generation, Country or Income Level

I know there are many authors who write for a particular generation such as Millennials, Generation Xers or other specific age groups. Others may focus on specific information related to a particular country, or certain income level. My book is intentionally 'not' geared to any particular group, geographic region or minimum income level.

When I was approached with the idea of writing a book, I wanted it to be the kind of material that would be valuable, regardless of any type of artificial boundary. After all, developing a positive financial mindset doesn't start or end at a particular age. Developing a spending plan works whether one earns $10,000 a year or $200,000. If someone has income, they can make use of the strategies outlined in the book. There are no limits to enjoying the "fruits" of sound financial management.

This Book is NOT a Get-Quick-Rich-Scheme

"Yeah, but Jay, have you seen the title of your book?" Yes, I'm quite aware of the title. In fact, I came up with it myself. But please don't confuse the concept of "*Fast Track to Prosperity*" with a "Get-Quick-Rich Scheme." If you are looking at making thousands, or millions, of dollars (Pesos, Yen, Euros, etc.) in a very short period of time, you will be sorely disheartened with this writing. There are many scams, frauds and schemes disguised as legitimate investments out there, so PLEASE be careful.

The concept of "Fast Track" means that by taking advantage of my life experiences, and the multitude of others that have participated in the Financial Literacy Program, your road to prosperity may be shorter than it would be without these learnings.

This Book is NOT Written by Someone with No Academic Credentials

You may look at my credentials and think, "Okay, this guy has a few letters after his name, so he must know something." But if truth be told, I am aware of a lot of people with more degrees after their name than a thermometer, but who know very little about the way things work in the real world. I'm sure you can think of a few also. So, what qualifies me to impart teaching to you?

Well, let's look at it another way. Suppose we got letters after our name for disappointments and failures in life rather than just accomplishments. I'd probably have a Graduate degree in F-O-O-L-I-S-H and a PhD. in G-U-I-L-L-I-B-L-E.

So, even though I have some credentials, the thing that qualifies me to teach you something is my life experiences coupled with my educational training. I know what it's like go through deep financial stress because of stupid decisions. I know what it's like to feel there is no hope, just money shame. I know what it feels to be at the darkest point in your life, where nothing matters. And while there is no such thing as a "do-over" in life, once a day is gone, it's gone. The next best thing I wish for you, is to learn from my experiences.

What the Book Will Do for You

I've spent some considerable time outlining what this book is NOT. Let me share a few thoughts on what it CAN do for you. Over the last four decades, I've learned some valuable lessons about finances, and of course, about life. Through these experiences, I've developed a simple process to fast track you to prosperity.

I know that when I talk about "prosperity," this means different things to different people. In the context of this writing, I am referring to "prosperity" in financial terms. I am acutely aware that prosperity entails more than money and material things. It is all relative and measured by the beholder. What one person considers "prosperous," another may desire more…or less. Only "YOU" can determine for yourself, what prosperity means to you. Don't let others make that decision for you.

My three-step process is **PAUSE, PLAN, and finally PROSPER**.

In the **PAUSE** section, you will learn:

- Why financial literacy is important and what financial bucket do you fall in
- How teachable you are when it comes to personal finances

- What are your core values around money and how those values could affect every financial decision you make?
- The importance of developing a wealthy mindset and practicing financial and lifestyle goal-setting
- Measuring and establishing your current financial position

In the **PLAN** section, you will learn:

- How Money Shame can sabotage your road to Prosperity
- Recognizing the many triggers that cause you to overspend
- Why Budgeting doesn't work and how developing a Spending Plan does
- How to make the Spending Plan work for you

Finally, in the **PROSPER** section, you will learn:

- The proper way to handle credit
- Getting out of Debt
- The path to investing
- Using Tax-assisted investments to reach your financial goals
- How to save hundreds of dollars a month so you never have to say "No" to that extra guacamole or that "double cheese" on your pizza

As a financial educator, I feel the best way to learn is not just read or listen, but to DO. There's nothing like applying knowledge to practice for reinforcing a concept, principle or to establish a positive habit. Therefore, at the end of most chapters, you will find some action steps to help you "crystalize" the content.

Although I believe I've included as much information as possible to have you complete the three-step-process, I have also made available some complimentary bonuses and gifts to those who would like some additional information, and action steps and forms in electronic format. These extras can be found throughout some of the chapters.

I am often asked, "How long does it take to see results?" Like any program, process or goal, the sooner one gets to it and sticks with it, the sooner the results can come to fruition. Of course, every person is different, and each situation unique. Success will depend on one's commitment, attitude, and most importantly, ACTION.

Having coached many students in the Financial Literacy Program, positive results can be achieved in as little as a few months. If you can take some time to PAUSE and take stock of your mindset, goals and where you're at, the next step is to PLAN. This is where you take control of your spending. And, now that you have some extra money left at the end of the month, you can begin to PROSPER with proper investing.

I used this exact process to lift me up from potential financial disaster. Regardless of your current financial situation, I am confident that applying the concepts and principles that many of my students and I have, you too may Fast Track your way to Prosperity.

Finally, as an Educator, Accountant and Money Coach, I use many student and client stories in this book that provide a look into the financial lives of everyday people. And while all these accounts are based on true experiences, the names have been changed to protect individual privacy. In addition, all the stories in the book are told with the express permission of the individuals who inspired them.

INTRODUCTION

On the first day of the Financial Literacy Program (FLP), I always start the session by asking my students a simple question. "How many of you here have ever made a poor financial mistake or a financial decision you wish you could take back?" I start by putting my hand up, and slowly a sea of hands go up all over the room. All of us have made them… some minor ones and maybe some more material ones as I've done. Let me share.

It was 2007, the global economy was humming with world stock markets rising and real estate values increasing all over the place. A friend of mine told me about an investment he was following and knew of some people who were already receiving good returns from it. It was called FOREX trading, where foreign currencies like American dollars and Euros are bought and sold for profit. FOREX trading is one of the riskiest investments one can make, but there is also potential for high returns. Certainly not for the faint at heart!

Nonetheless, I reviewed the information that was sent to me. A friend of mine and I even flew out to meet the individual who began marketing the investment in Canada. I considered myself very thorough and always performed my due diligence before putting any of my money down. We asked many questions about how the funds were traded, where the traders resided in New York and the potential risks. Some responses were acceptable, while others were less than adequate. Nonetheless, after my friend and I met with the representative, we were even more convinced about the legitimacy and opportunity before us.

I started with the minimum investment of $3,000 and awaited eagerly as the weekly statement came out every Tuesday morning showing the weekly gains. Some days there were profits while others had losses, but we were making about 7-10% gains on our investment every week. I even made a small withdrawal to make sure I could get my money out, and it worked. Wow! I figured I had hit the jackpot. What an easy way to make money, I thought.

After a few months of consistently high returns, I decided to invest even more money into the newfound venture. I was so confident of the opportunity that I started sharing this with family and friends. I proudly showed them my weekly statements and the slick charts displaying unbelievable returns. They got caught up in the same frenzy I experienced and knowing someone like myself who had already experienced success made it all the more credible. My contacts started putting in thousands and some, even hundreds of thousands of dollars into the deal.

I was encouraged by their faith and the large amounts they were throwing into this deal. The more I thought about it, the more I felt I was foregoing some huge profits. Call it greed or the fear of missing out, I wasn't going to be denied. So, there I was, ready to go all in.

The cash I had in my bank account was not nearly enough to the amount I was thinking of investing. In a few days, I made an appointment with my bank advisor and asked for a large loan. I applied for a home equity line of credit, also known as a HELOC. This is a loan where one borrows against the available equity in their home, and the house is used as collateral.

Definitely, it's a risky endeavor if you borrow, use the money for something and then don't have the funds to pay off the loan. The lender has the right to take your home and sell it to recover the money they lent you. But, I had such confidence in this venture and had no worries about applying for the HELOC. Without going into the details on the amount, let's just say that because real estate prices were rising all over, I was able to borrow a large amount of money against my home to invest.

It was mid-January of 2008, the weeks idling by, and I looked forward to the upcoming Tuesday update. That particular morning went by, and nothing arrived in my email inbox. It was strange, but the update came late a few times, so I was not panicking. Well, not yet anyway.

I think all of us can relate to moments in time when we hear about a surprising, emotional or important event. This could be a publicly significant event like where we were or what we were doing on September 11, 2001, when the world heard about the World Trade Center attack. Or when Princess Diana died in that fatal car crash in Paris in 1997. However, these types of memories are not limited to events that happen in the public domain. The same substantial impact can happen with significant events in our personal lives, like the sudden loss of a friend or getting bad news about your health.

I remember heading out from work to go grab some lunch at noon. It was a cold, wintery day in Canada. The snow-packed roads were slippery and the visibility was poor as exhaust from vehicles formed low-lying clouds in front of me. Not trying to think of the worst-case scenario, I called my friend who introduced me to the investment. He was just as perplexed about the absence of our weekly updates, but chalked it up to some minor disruption in the process.

I was somewhat relieved after talking to him, but the thought of what may have happened consumed me during my lunch hour. About a half-hour later, I received a call from my friend. He had just received some information that would forever change my life. There was news that a couple of principals, at the head of the FOREX trading company in New York, were arrested for defrauding hundreds of investors. He and his partner used investor money to pay for luxurious items and personal living expenses. A small amount of personal and company assets were frozen and seized by U.S. Authorities.

The Securities Exchange Commission (SEC), in New York, referred to the arrangement as a Ponzi scheme. This is one of the most common investment frauds, where new investors are enticed to put their money into an investment opportunity that promises high returns. Money put in by new investors is used to pay earlier investors who withdraw funds and think their investments are earning them the 'promised' returns. A similar plan was structured by Bernie Madoff, one of history's most notorious fraudsters, who ran the largest Ponzi scheme in history of about $65 billion USD the same year.

The company sent us investors false account statements reporting nonexistent trades and profits to conceal the scheme. So, all those charts and profit returns were manufactured to make it look like our investment was working for us, when in fact, it was all a scam.

Well, my heart sank! I felt like someone drove a stake through it. A flood of emotions ran through me as I tried to process what I had just heard. I was in shock at the recent developments. My thoughts immediately went to what this meant. Would I get any money back? If not, what did this mean for my financial future? How would this affect all my family and friends that invested in the scheme because of me?

The rest of the afternoon was a write-off at work. All I could focus on was what happened and my disbelief in the report. I started getting calls from family and friends inquiring about their missing statements, not having heard about the arrest. I told them what transpired that afternoon, and I could feel the pain, sorrow and disappointment in their reaction or the awkward silence on the other end of the phone.

The next several days weren't any better as more information about the arrests came to light. The more I learned about the scam, the more I worried about how this would end. It was no consolation to learn that many other investors, including celebrities and people much more intelligent than I, were also scammed by these con artists.

The following six months became one of the most challenging times in my life. Let's just say I went to a dark place that I never want to experience again. It took its toll and affected me physically, emotionally, spiritually and every other aspect of my well-being. I couldn't concentrate on anything but the current situation I found myself engulfed in. My personal financial state of affairs was secondary to the thought of that of my family, friends and their families. How many of them wished they had never met me? How much hardship did I cause them? Even though everyone is ultimately in control of their own financial decisions, and no one was forced to invest, I still felt personally responsible for introducing them to the opportunity. The thoughts in my mind ran wild.

The nights became sleepless. I would rest for a few hours before waking up, hoping it was just a bad nightmare, only to realize that no, it was real life I was experiencing. I couldn't go to work and was placed on medical leave for several months. Before this event, I prided myself on exercising regularly and being fit. Now, not only did I lack the energy, but I also just didn't care about how I looked or my overall health.

After a few trips to the emergency room at the hospital for both mental and physical issues, I knew I had to seriously tackle this if I was going to change the course of my life. I became a slave to my pessimistic state of mind. I often felt I was in a trance and wondered what purpose I had to go on living. This definitely affected my family life and I felt disconnected to those close to me.

Coming to terms with my current reality was difficult. After all, I had been strong and confident most of my life. I was successful and accomplished anything I set my mind to. Now, I was a shell of the confident man that I had been. What would others think of me after this? Would it show my vulnerability and weakness? How would it affect my relationship with them? Would their perception of me be diminished in their eyes? All emotions that I endlessly battled in my mind.

Finally, I was referred to a professional mental health practitioner by the medical doctor in my company. This started a slow and steady process towards recovery. The biggest obstacle I faced was that of money shame. This is the feeling of guilt, embarrassment and humiliation one places on themselves for making poor financial decisions. I've devoted several parts of the book to this subject because I know many individuals struggle with this emotion.

I then worked on slowly getting my confidence back. My counsellor had me recall and journal all the successes I had experienced before this event. Over the next several months, I progressed to the point where my mental state improved. I also began exercising again, and I was able to "see the light" at the end of the proverbial "tunnel."

To make a very long story shorter, during this period of recovery, I started to develop a process that would eventually lift me from the depths of despair that this financial mistake had catapulted me into. I needed to **PAUSE, PLAN,** and ultimately, I would **PROSPER.** I will go into the details of these key steps and the exact process I used throughout the book.

In the **PAUSE** stage, I stopped the negative thinking that was dragging me down and took stock of where I was. Just like rebooting a computer or a cell phone, I reset the "factory settings" in my mind so I could think clearly and find a solution to my current situation. I reconnected to my financial and personal core values and set short, medium and longer-term goals.

The second part of the process, the **PLAN,** was the mechanics of the system. This is where I applied myself to take total control of my finances. It was the most challenging element to complete. All the positive thinking and gaining knowledge of finances would not have mattered without action.

With the two steps "under my belt" and my action plan in motion, I was able to **PROSPER**. For me, this meant recovering from my financially disastrous decision. Just as important was sustaining this result. It was critical to the process, and the work and actions from the first two stages continue to **PROSPER** me to this very day. And I'll share with you how I've been able to do this.

Since that time, I've taught this same system to hundreds of participants in the Financial Literacy Program (FLP), college students, and individual money coaching sessions. The three (3) step process is simple to follow, and I promise that by the time you finish reading this book, you will, **Fast Track to Prosperity**.

Finally, I believe that the best way to learn and make progress in your financial journey is to take action. To that end, as you go through this book, you will find Action Steps at the end of most chapters. I want you to benefit from my life experiences, failures and successes and immediately start implementing those steps in your life. Doing so will help ensure success and assist you in achieving your financial goals and priorities much sooner. I've compiled a companion workbook that includes exercises, checklists and other beneficial material that relate to the Action Steps.

This workbook is my gift to you that you can download at
www.fasttrack2prosperity.com/bonus
Or scan this QR code with your phone camera.

SECTION ONE – PAUSE

A YOUNG KID'S VENTURE INTO THE ICE-CREAM SELLING WORLD

Ready to move on from delivering newspapers door to door, I was keen on getting a job with more hours during my summer off from school. At the ripe old age of thirteen, I thought I'd try my hand at selling ice cream. After all, I had been eating it all my life; how hard could it be? This wasn't like selling out of a Baskins-Robbins or Yogen-Fruz storefront, complete with air conditioning and backed up with a well-oiled franchising system. No, this was selling ice cream out of a cart with a less than padded bicycle seat and three wheels on long, hot summer days.

The city was dominated by one large vendor called "Dickie-Dee". Always being a fan of the underdog and somewhat intimidated by Dickie-Dee's slick marketing and more rugged fellow ice-cream peddlers, I joined their competition. "Chilly-Willy" was the "new kid on the block." They had smoother-looking carts, a totally different line of ice cream and the mascot was a cool-looking penguin. I was all in. Sign me up!

I showed up at the "Chilly-Willy" headquarters in an old brick warehouse. I hadn't seen so many ice cream carts in one place. Dozens of teens would sit in line, and like cars being manufactured on an assembly line, they slowly moved up, one by one, to get their lot of ice cream for the day before venturing out.

After a couple of days of training and some follow-alongs, I was finally set to tackle the world of dispensing frozen treats to the world on my own. We could ride anywhere in the city to sell our ice cream, but I quickly learned that the farther I went from headquarters, the longer the distance back at the end of the night. Nothing worse than knowing you had miles of riding back after a long and hot summer day.

On this particular day, I set up shop a few kilometers away from our office and made some brisk sales with young children scurrying to my ice cream cart. Nothing more exciting for a kid and some older kids at heart, to see the varied selection and finally making their choice. As I was waiting for some more customers, I noticed another cart coming towards me: a "Dickie-Dee" bike. He rode up to me and asked, "What are you doing here?" I fought to control my sarcasm as we both stood there sitting on ice cream carts. Nonetheless, I gave way to caution, a couple of years of age older than me and 30 pounds and said nothing. He then proceeded to say that I was on his territory and that I needed to leave immediately.

My two days of training quickly passed before my eyes as I desperately tried to recall anything about territorial rights. Came up with nothing. Was it like when animals mark their territories? No, I didn't see a sign, fence, or "Dickie-Dee" ice cream drippings around a perimeter that would signal I was in someone's space. Coming up blank, I thought I was working in a free country and could sell my wares anywhere except on private property. We stood there exchanging remarks back and forth, but I was clearly starting to get intimidated by this older kid.

I saw another teen on a bike approaching us within a few minutes. As he got closer, he seemed to get larger and larger, and so did the "Dickie-Dee" logo on his t-shirt. I knew this person; he came from a family of five brothers. He got off his bike, and like a sergeant dismounting his horse, walked over with the authority of an ice cream czar. He asked the other kid what was going on and was given an explanation of the situation. This guy was over six feet tall and built like a brick house and, by the way, went on to play semi-pro football a few years later. He stood there looking mean and with the body language of "The Rock". I obviously felt bullied that day, and he proceeded to tell me that I could sell anywhere except where I was.

I wasn't about to argue with these two aggressors as I valued my young life and knew my mother was cooking my favorite pasta that night. I could not miss that. The older kid asked me to follow him, and I complied. Like a foreign airplane being escorted by a fighter jet from restricted airspace, I trailed the “Dickie-Dee” ice-cream police out of their self-proclaimed territory.

I finished the rest of the shift and then went home, contemplating the events of the day. The thought of telling my superiors at “Chilly-Willy” or my parents what transpired didn’t cross my mind. I guess I had two choices: either quit for the summer and go back to delivering newspapers or take time to **PAUSE** and think how I would sell more ice cream.

1

THE FINANCIAL LANDSCAPE

To say there has been a vast difference in my generation compared to that of my parents is a colossal understatement. As I look back at even the last 10-15 years, I realize my son will never be able to relate to things like a VCR (some of you may have to Google this). Or experience the disappointment of making a trip to a video store with hundreds of selections on the shelf only to find the last available copy of the newest release snatched by Johnny and his mother. My son will never experience the pleasure of going to a music store to flip through the vinyl records before buying them.

The differences in the financial landscape are just as pronounced. The personal story I shared in the previous chapter, and my teaching and coaching of hundreds of folks, have led me to a conclusion.

I believe our personal financial knowledge is not keeping pace with the vast financial maze in today's world currently faced by individuals.

We are continuously being bombarded with information on finances. Buy stocks, invest in mutual funds, save for retirement and kid's education…oh yeah, and buy real estate (but be careful where you buy). And if you have a house, pay off the mortgage first instead of putting money in your retirement account. Instead of buying real estate, just rent and invest that money. You'll be better off. Trying to keep up with the latest thoughts from all the financial "advisors and experts" is just as confusing as the health claims that litter our daily lives from the internet, TV, radio and general conversation. Everybody is an expert these days.

You know what I mean. One day the latest study suggests that you should avoid that particular superfood or drink at any cost and then six months later, guess what? There's a conflicting study from another prestigious University saying just the opposite. Okay, should we assume this latest finding is the best information or rely on the previous data? This is where it becomes baffling for many people.

Governments: Not the Best Example of Sound Financial Management

Unfortunately, when it comes to finances, many countries worldwide are not setting a good example. There are record deficits, insurmountable debt, poor or non-existent regulations for banks, not to mention the political corruption that has financial implications on citizens, and so on. I can't help but think that these substandard financial patterns set by governments around the world may be a reflection, and an extension, of our own personal finances. Governments continue to run deficits such as spending more on programs, services, etc. than they take in from tax revenues. To fund the deficits and pay the interest costs, they just borrow more money from some source and thereby continue to amass even more debt.

This is not a Political Science course, but I think many would agree that there is a lack of accountability for politicians. Their ultimate goal is to remain in power and to do this, they need our vote. How do they get our vote? They provide tax breaks, incentives, give in to special interest groups and spend our money. It is no coincidence that the larger the voting block of individuals or businesses (who can provide handsome political contributions at election time), the more the government gives in to their requests and demands. Often, this is at the expense of the taxpayer and the citizen.

I remember when millions of dollars being spent by a government seemed like a lot. Over the last several years, *billions* entered our conversation. Does anyone find it disturbing that now governments are spending *trillions* of dollars? Who will pay for this? We know the answer... We, the taxpayers, through higher taxes, fewer services, reduced education and health care funding, etc. And if the debt isn't eliminated in our lifetime, well then our children and generations to come will inherit the debt load.

According to a recent article in the Visual Capitalist, the U.S. national debt is $27 trillion.[1] That's with a capital "T." Of the G7 countries, the governments with the highest debt, as a percentage of GDP (Gross Domestic Product), are Japan at 257%, followed by Italy at 157%. This means that Japan's debt is more than two and a half times the monetary value of all goods and services produced by them as a country for the year (GDP.) Similarly, Italy's is one and a half times their GDP. Definitely not an example of sound debt management.

Definition:

G7 countries - A group of 7 countries that represent the largest and most advanced countries in the world.

In contrast, if you and I were to spend more money than we took in every month...month after month, year after year and simply borrow, getting further into debt, where would we end up? At some point in time, our income would not even cover the interest on the debt, which means that we would end up in financial ruin.

How about if every time someone in the family wanted something, we gave in to the request regardless of the cost? After all, we didn't have it growing up as kids, so now I want my little Jesse to enjoy what I missed out on.

We are inundated with slick marketing, which leads us to believe that we can (and should) have anything we want. And not into the future, but NOW! In fact, we are all aware of how we can use our mobile phone to place an order online (I won't mention the name of the company here as they don't need any extra promotion). Next-day delivery ensures I get that *Hamburger Press Patty* maker, because my life wouldn't be the same without this plastic kitchen gadget. I can't believe I used my hands to make patties all these years, but now I can look forward to ensuring each patty is perfectly uniform!

To be clear, I'm not against consumption as a means of acquiring and using goods and services to meet our needs. I like owning the latest technology, buying quality clothes, and having more dress-shirts for work than I care to iron. But, I'm also seeing a disturbing trend in consumerism and overconsumption. This is where companies go to lengths to try and meet our emotional and social needs through shopping and defining our self-worth through "stuff."

If we just continue to mount debt, give in to every impulsive purchase and have no regard to controlling this, we would undoubtedly be on a path to financial disaster.

For a recent commentary on consumer debt, The State of Household Debt in America, notes that U.S. household debt has doubled from $7.23 trillion in 2003 to $14.56 trillion in 2020.[2] With just under 130 million households, that equates to an average of $118,000 (USD) of debt per household. And interesting to cite, student loan debt as a category has expanded the most at a colossal 550% in the same time period.

The Canadian scene does not fare well either. Canadian consumers are carrying $1.47 trillion (USD) debt. With just over 10.3 million households, it equates to an average of $142,000 (USD) of debt per household.[3] A survey by MNP, one of the largest accounting agencies in Canada, found that over half (53%) of Canadian households were $200 or less away from insolvency.[4] This means that the person is unable to meet the financial obligations of paying lenders on time.

Part of the reason for the increased debt load amongst people is the accepted practice of carrying debt by governments, an increase and instant gratification of our wants, and a long and steady period of low interest rates. Individuals don't consider the impact of the debt and the cost of borrowing, but rather how much can I afford to borrow and make reasonable payments? The most concerning part of these scenarios is that just a tiny increase in interest rates can make a big difference in payments and spell financial disaster for many families.

And just in case we think this applies only to folks in distressed financial situations, this is the profile of many families and individuals I've met with. We live in times where this debt crisis is considered normal.

It was rare in the 1950s and 1960s for an individual to be in foreclosure or file for bankruptcy. By 2018, in an average neighborhood in the U.S., for every 100 mortgages, there was at least one foreclosure and another three seriously delinquent ones.[5] These late or delinquent accounts are typically 3 or more months behind, and the data doesn't even consider missing a payment on the due date or 30 and 60 days behind because it is so common. I would venture to guess that some of these borrowers are finding it difficult to juggle their debt and are routinely late on payments. What would happen if an unplanned emergency reared its ugly head? Maybe a car repair, home maintenance, or personal family emergency requiring travel on short notice? Any of these events could easily slip an already delinquent payer into the foreclosure category.

It used to be that the only time people borrowed money was when making a large purchase like a home. In the 1960s, this was common and understandable, as home prices were steadily climbing. By the end of the 60s and into the 1970s, credit cards arrived on the scene, and people started to be comfortable with the idea of using credit to purchase consumer goods.

Well, since then, credit card companies have been on "steroids" with their polished marketing, product offerings, classes of cards and of course, those all-important "points". More to come on that in the final part of the book. These financial companies are raking in huge profits coming primarily through the interest charges they collect on balances that are not fully paid. Different interest rates are levied depending on the type of card and individual credit rating. According to Wallethub, an online financial management tool, in 2021, these can range from approximately 13% to 24%.[6] You may want to take note of how much banks are paying us for interest on our savings account balances to realize the huge penalty we pay for unpaid credit card balances. In addition, if you do manage to pay your credit card balance monthly, the companies continue to raise your credit limit to entice you to spend more.

To see the effect on a society where credit is easy to obtain and debt is considered normal, recent data from the Federal Reserve's Survey of Consumer Finances reveals our situation. The 2019 average credit card debt in America was $6,270.[7] It's important to note that this is ONLY consumer credit card debt and does not include debt on a mortgage or other individual loans from banks.

There are several issues associated with this consumer credit crisis. Not only are we buying more "stuff" we may not necessarily need. But, because credit is easily available, many are also paying ridiculously high-interest costs for not paying credit card balances in full when due.

Now, I don't want to leave you with the impression that it's "gloom and doom" and that we're in this large spinning drum going round and round, and because of centrifugal force, must give in and accept our fate. Great… I just got an image of me in a washing machine! There is hope if we apply sound principles, starting with increasing our financial literacy.

Financial Literacy: What is it?

Financial literacy can be described as reading for knowledge and thinking critically about financially related material. Furthermore, if this knowledge is applied correctly, it enables a person to make sensible short and long-term financial decisions.

Financial literacy is not just about knowledge; it is also about attitude and behavior, which we will see in the upcoming sections and chapters.

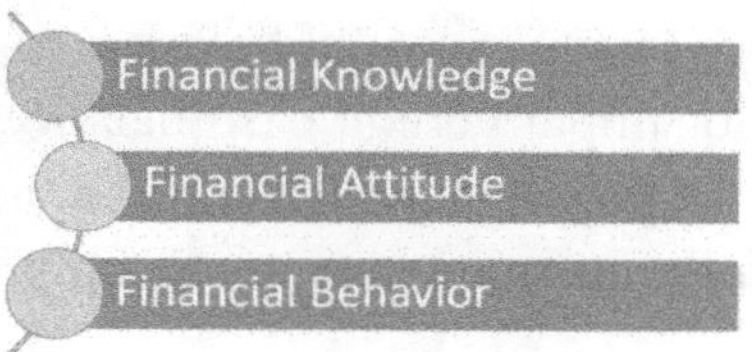

The financial landscape is vast and encompasses so many subjects and areas that one never "arrives" at being totally financially literate. Sure, there are experts in various categories like the stock market, real estate, or even making money online, but rarely is someone proficient at everything.

Warren Buffet, one of the world's most successful value investors and a multi-billionaire, obviously is a master in this area. Still, I would venture to think that he's probably not up to the same level of knowledge regarding cryptocurrencies or real estate.

As such, gaining financial knowledge is a lifelong, intellectual process. It consists of acquiring this by reading, attending courses and seminars or listening to financial material. And of course, also through personal experience.

One of the weekly assignments I have students complete in both Levels 1 and 2 of the Financial Literacy Program (FLP) I instruct is called "Being in Tune with Financial Literacy". The intent of the exercise is to get participants to develop a habit of listening, watching or reading business-related news. They are asked to briefly summarize the subject's content and, most importantly, how if any of their learnings apply to them personally. I tell them that if they are persistent, little by little, their financial knowledge will grow.

And by the end of the two-month program, they are in a better position to make sense of a variety of financially related material.

Some examples of headlines we've looked at included the following:

▸ The Bank of America is set to increase its service fees by 10%

- So what does this mean if you bank there?
- Should you be looking at changing banks or, at the very least, see if there are lower fee bank account options?
- Should you consider investing in Bank of America stock?

▸ Statistics Canada reports that March's CPI (Consumer Price Index) rose by 4.3% compared to March of last year.

- Is this an anomaly or a trend that you need to watch?
- Did you notice paying higher for gas, groceries, etc.? Do you need to do some better planning/or budgeting around monthly expenses?

▸ The Finance Minister reports that families are carrying record-setting debt and that a slight increase in interest rates could spell disaster for many households.

- What is your debt load?
- Do you know the amount of each debt and the interest you're paying on it?
- How would a one percentage point increase in the interest rate affect your finances?

- Do you need to put a more aggressive debt repayment plan in place?

▸ Apple's share prices increased 4% on news that net income for the quarter increased by 10% with the launch of the next iPhone.

- Is it time to evaluate Apple and buy stock?
- Is it time to take some profits "off the table" from your investment if you have Apple stock?

The exercise is graded, and we start the classes with a few students sharing what they've learned from business news. It is so satisfying to see the quality and responses in the assignment increase as we go through the program. At the end of the semester, I strongly encourage them to continue the habit of listening to the business news to further increase their literacy. Feedback from the participants is that they can now listen and hear about business headlines and make sense of what's being reported.

The Education System

I think it's quite common to hear the notion that the education system does not prepare children well enough to succeed in the financial world. And this is not a "knock" on our teachers. Most of my family are teachers. Brother, sister-in-law and four cousins. A couple are principals, and all of them are dedicated and seasoned professionals who take their job seriously and have the best interest of students in mind.

But if you think of one skill that we need as adults, that we use every day, it's making sense of financial concepts. We're making financial decisions every day. We get up in the morning and decide, "Am I going to make my lunch, or should I buy it?" Later on, I may go online and pay my monthly bills. Then I go shopping, and even though I'm buying groceries, it may not seem like a consequential decision, but it is a financial decision, right?

No offense to the math teachers out there, but in addition to math, social studies, English and the sciences, why don't we add financial literacy to prepare these kids better for adulthood? I know certain schools are starting to offer some financial teachings at the High School level, but this won't suffice! We need to start teaching these essential concepts and skills at the elementary stage and then into the more advanced grades so that when these young kids finish school, they can manage money. We can all agree this is an area of knowledge that many of us as adults wish we had been taught more about throughout our years of schooling.

Tammy G, 24*. Yeah, I remember taking a CALM (Career and Life Management) class in high school and it was good, but it was like 3 Chapters, hardly enough to get me started in managing my finances. I learned how to open a bank account and how to apply for a credit card but that's about it. It would have been nice to learn about bank fees, what type of account I should have, how debt works and about interest rates…that would have been more helpful.*

Let's treat finances like any one of the other core subjects. It shouldn't be an elective where we leave it to a child to choose but make it a compulsory subject. I am also aware that colleges and universities now offer personal finance courses. I have taught these courses at this level as a requirement for certain business-related degrees and diplomas. Unfortunately, they had to be cancelled several times when offered as a separate course due to lack of interest.

BUT….there is hope. I am encouraged that financial

education has gained a prominent position in the global policy agenda and is universally recognized as a core component of financial empowerment. There are many initiatives, at various levels, including central banks, financial regulators, ministries of finance and education, and these are having a positive impact on financial literacy worldwide.

So, Where Do Adults Fit in with Financial Knowledge?

Financial knowledge is probably the most critical element of financial literacy. The key for carrying out activities such as following news about the economic and financial environment, assessing financial products, services and investments and making sound financial decisions. Basic knowledge of financial concepts and numbers allows individuals to make personal decisions and effectively manage their finances.

Over the last several years of money coaching, I've seen that higher levels of financial knowledge are often associated with positive outcomes. Stock market and real estate investing, participation and planning for retirement, and reduction in debt are good examples of this.

Are you surprised when you hear of celebrities or professional athletes that have enjoyed multimillion-dollar contracts or made millions over the life of their careers, and now they're either bankrupt or in a financial crisis?

My father would always say that it's not about the money you make...it's about what you keep and invest in.

I'm not surprised. We can all make mistakes, have a lapse of judgment, or sometimes it's just the nature of risk with investments, but when individuals continue to exercise poor financial habits, it can spell ruin. So, it's not necessarily dependent on how much money one makes but **how** they manage what they do earn.

So, if sound financial habits are essential, how do we measure financial literacy? There's no standard body of knowledge that you can test someone against. And as stated, financial literacy encompasses so much that it would be difficult to assess. There are, however, several surveys and studies out there that attempt to do just that.

The 2017 Organization for Economic Co-operation and Development (OECD) Survey on G20/OECD Report on Adult Financial literacy in G20 measured respondents' financial knowledge, attitudes and behaviors. It is interesting to see how they measure and compare financial literacy amongst various countries as an international body.

This particular research concluded that **many people do not have basic financial knowledge**. On average, across G20 countries, fewer than half of adults (48%) could answer 70% of the financial knowledge questions correctly (the minimum target score).

Definition:

G20 countries - A group of 20 countries that represent the largest and most advanced countries and economies in the world.

In particular, understanding the concept of diversification and compounding is weak. These two concepts are essential for people to recognize the consequences of financial decisions, such as paying the minimum repayment on credit cards and managing their increasing responsibility for financial security in retirement. Four in ten people did not understand diversification, and only 27% of respondents were able to both calculate simple interest and recognize the added benefit of compounding over five years.[8]

I went and looked up the survey and thought I'd complete

it. I'll be honest, I was a bit reluctant because I figured I had better at least pass this (lol). After reviewing the survey, I thought the questions were quite basic and more common sense rather than having a solid base of financial knowledge.

I couldn't help but think that if someone took the quiz and got 60 percent, which was the minimum score, would they have enough skills to navigate through the financial maze out there and effectively manage their money? The answer is a resounding NO!

A fundamental understanding is not enough. Let me ask you something… When you get on a plane, do you want that pilot to have just a BASIC understanding of how to fly? Or do you want someone with some experience, knowledge, and knowhow to handle any uncommon issue that might come arise?

How about your doctor? Are you comfortable with one that has just a BASIC understanding of a condition? Or do you want your physician to have extensive experience, up on the latest developments and more? That's why we shouldn't be satisfied with any survey that says that an average score is enough for us to manage our finances.

Every time I read the results of a survey or study; I'm always interested in what the questions are. We all know you can make the statistics "dance" in your favor depending on how one collects and reports the information.

The Three Financial Knowledge Buckets

I've seen people fall into one of three buckets when it comes to financial knowledge. There's bucket number one, the financially literate. As we've discussed, they can read or listen to financial data, interpret, and make decisions that positively impact their financial position.

Then there's bucket number two. These individuals understand the importance of being financially literate. Still, they feel that it is either too complicated and not for them, or it's easier to let someone else do it for them. At times, it's a partner or spouse, and other times can be a financial advisor, accountant or bank employee that will save them from having to take personal control and responsibility of their finances.

And finally, the third bucket. This is the category that is the most "financially dangerous." These folks "think" they have financial knowledge but clearly do not. I'm sure we all know that person that "knows" everything, but "they don't know what they don't know". These individuals can't be taught anything...let's just say their Teachability Index (TI) is lower than a snake's belly in a ditch. More about this in a later chapter.

Yes, Financial Literacy Is Important

As discussed earlier, we all make financial decisions of varying importance every day. In some cases, our choices today can significantly impact our future and those of our families. The cost of financial stress on individuals is real. FP Canada, a national professional body that certifies professional financial planners, released a Financial Stress Index to help gauge this vital aspect of our lives. Two in five Canadians say that money is their number one stress.[9] Even amid a pandemic, money outranked personal health for the fourth consecutive time. Interestingly enough, money (ahead of personal health), work and relationships are causing the most stress. The Index also highlights that the impacts of this financial stress led to personal health, family, relationship and lower productivity issues.

2021 Financial Stress Index

Two-in-five Canadians say money is their #1 source of stress

Even amid a public health crisis, money outranked personal health for the fourth consecutive time

What's causing Canadians the most stress?

Money
38%

Personal Health
26%

Work
20%

Relationships
15%

Summary

In this chapter, we defined and learned about the importance of Financial Literacy. There is so much financial information out there that if we don't have a good understanding of personal finances, we are bound to make poor or somewhat suboptimal decisions.

Financial literacy includes not only the knowledge base, but attitude and behavior, which can equally have a significant impact on a person's financial situation.

Above all, we should not look to our governments for leadership in managing and controlling finances. Their model is to over-promise so they can get re-elected. By virtue of the massive debts they have amassed, they do not consider the financial implications of overextending debt.

Financial decisions play an essential role in our daily lives yet have not been well integrated into our education system. As such, many kids have to learn about finances on their own or from not the best sources. This can lead to poor decisions or learning about finances from trial and error.

Financial literacy is difficult to assess, but international research suggests that most people do not have adequate knowledge to make sound financial decisions. It is encouraging to see that some global financial literacy initiatives have sprung up in recent years. This will undoubtedly help young people gain more knowledge in the education system and help adults worldwide.

The Financial Landscape
Action Step

Go to the *Fast Track to Prosperity Workbook* to answer questions about which group (financial bucket) you consider yourself to be in and why you chose this response?

This exercise can be found at
www.fasttrack2prosperity.com/bonus
Or scan this QR code with your phone camera.

2

HOW IT ALL STARTED

Fort McMurray, Alberta is a small city nestled in the North-Western part of Canada. It sits in the Regional Municipality of Wood Buffalo, which by area, is one of the largest municipalities in North America. We are proud to have five First Nation bands and 6 Metis groups represented in the region. The city is located in the middle of the Athabasca oil sands. Many have come far and wide for the opportunity to work in this oil and gas hub. Although small relative to other cities, Fort McMurray is a multi-cultural melting pot with over 60 different countries represented in the region.

Let me provide a little background on how we started the Financial Literacy program (FLP). It was early 2013, and because I worked in the oil and gas industry, I was asked to speak to an English Language class for new Canadians at the local College. These students were recently new to Canada and were either already working in a job or hoping to gain future employment. But all were there with one common goal: to improve their English. The College had asked me to talk about how to land a "prized" job with any of the oil and gas companies, prepare for an interview, and share any tips that would help give them a greater likelihood of obtaining employment.

After my introduction, I asked the students to go around the room and introduce themselves to break the ice. As part of their introduction, they were to share with the group: the country they arrived from, say welcome in their native language, and tell one thing they appreciated about their new home here in Canada. As they went around the room, the list of countries represented started to mount: India, Thailand, Colombia, China, Syria, Guatemala, Brazil, Egypt, Pakistan, Ukraine and so on. As each student proudly announced their country of origin, I knew those geography skills I developed in grade school would finally come in handy. As I crisscrossed the globe with every country mentioned, I envisioned their homeland and marveled at how far they had travelled to get to Canada.

When it came to the question of what they appreciated about Canada, let's just say I wasn't emotionally prepared for some of their responses. There were short replies about fleeing refugee camps, being in physical danger, not having hope and seeking a better future for themselves and their children. It was hard to keep my composure as I listened to each participant and wondered how every person represented had such a unique story of their journey here.

Fortunately, we got to the part where they said "welcome" in their native tongue, and that quickly broke the tension from some of their heart-wrenching responses. The entire class roared with good-natured laughter at my attempt at a few of the languages as I welcomed them to Canada in their mother tongue. I could hold my own on some of the Romance languages, but when it came to the Asian and Middle Eastern ones, I was stumped.

After the introductions, I proceeded with my presentation on getting employment and answered their many questions. I could feel a warm connection to the class, and the students started to open up about the many challenges faced by new immigrants. They mentioned the new language, a different culture, a harsher climate, and the pressures of finding employment to make ends meet. A few of them had established careers and formal education in their home country. Still, they would have to take exams and get practical experience in Canada to resume their professions. Engineers, doctors, lawyers, and accountants. The road ahead was about to get long and arduous for many of them.

On top of that, they commented on the financial maze that they had to navigate through. A new banking system, definitely a new income tax system, credit ratings and scores, and so on. As I listened to their concerns, I could only feel for the difficulty ahead for my newfound friends related to financial matters.

I pondered their dilemma and thought there was certainly a need in the community to help these new citizens to our beautiful and prosperous region. I had some friends involved with the local Multicultural Association, and I contacted them with the idea to provide financial literacy to newcomers. Although many new immigrant resources existed, this essential financial information source was missing.

We developed a program that covered the following basic topics of financial literacy:

- Banking
- Budgeting
- Income Taxes
- Credit
- Investments
- Insurance
- Government-sponsored programs
- Fraud and personal financial security

The Multicultural Association of Wood Buffalo (MCAWB) received some funding for the program from United Way, and the intent was to offer the sessions at no cost. We started marketing the program and, for the first couple of offerings, only a handful of attendees came out. Well, word must have spread or maybe it was because it was free (lol), but soon we were getting the maximum of 30 participants per class and even had to start a waiting list. We definitely felt we were meeting a much-needed service in the community.

We would celebrate at the end of the two-month program with a short graduation ceremony and a potluck meal. Each student would bring a traditional dish from their country, and we enjoyed a great meal together. It was tremendously encouraging to see these students finish the program and see the pride of accomplishment as they walked up to accept their certificate of completion.

At the end of every program offering, participants would provide an evaluation to incorporate their feedback and improve the program. I thought at some point, someone would recommend "replace the instructor", but fortunately, that didn't happen…not even once. And just in case you're wondering, no, I did not collect the evaluations, they went straight to the Association staff. (Lol)

In all seriousness, participants were very grateful for the Financial Literacy Program and commented on how much they had learned and wanted to keep learning to gain additional financial knowledge. They said the basics were excellent, but many wanted to learn more complex financial skills, such as picking stocks and investing in real estate.

By this time, I had started my company Prospero Financial Solutions Ltd. which provided money coaching to individuals and financial literacy training to small and medium-sized companies. I further developed more advanced material and came up with Level 2 of the Financial Literacy program. Topics included:

- The value of money and financial goal setting
- Determining and controlling your finances
- How to pick stocks
- How to evaluate a private offering
- Real Estate investing
- Multiple streams of income and
- Cryptocurrencies

Again, we went out and marketed the Program and were getting a maximum number of participants signing up with a waiting list. But what we found was that the program was not only attracting new immigrants to Canada, but many local Canadians. And what brought me great joy over the last several semesters: more high school students signing up.

Both Levels 1 and 2 of the Financial Literacy Program continue to be offered twice a year, with hundreds of participants attending each year. Even during the pandemic, other than the spring of 2020, we took every extra precaution and still held live sessions. In the next chapter, I want to share how I prepare students to learn.

3

WHAT'S YOUR TEACHABILITY INDEX (TI)?

Several years ago, I attended some personal development training where I was introduced to an interesting concept called the "Teachability Index". It had such a significant impact on me that, I still apply it to my daily life to this very day. However, before I start explaining it, you're probably thinking: What does teaching, teachability or an index have to do with financial literacy?

Well, my key point here is that **whenever we're trying**

to make any type of change, whether it's learning a new skill for work or the home, trying to develop a positive habit in our lives, or even trying to find a new way to manage our finances, we need to get brutally honest about what is holding us back from changing.

In this personal development class, the facilitator went around the room and asked a few of us, "are you teachable?" I thought it was such an odd question considering we all spent a pretty penny to attend the training. Everybody enthusiastically and confidently nodded, "yes." I mean, what else are you going to say in a room full of people you don't know and where you just want the instructor to "get on with it"?

As the facilitator started explaining the model and I further appreciated what it meant, I could not help but think of the hundreds of times I wasn't ready and primed to learn.

The concept behind the teachability index illustrates that most people think of themselves as good learners but are not easily teachable and coachable. Many people read and may know the theories but have a hard time applying them to their daily lives. Or, they "have heard it all before" but can never make that transition of actually doing something with what they have learned.

As per the cartoon at the beginning of the chapter, there's a joke that goes, "I'm opening a gym called *Resolutions*. It will have exercise equipment in it for the first two weeks, and then it turns into a bar for the remainder of the year." It is not a lack of knowledge; it is applying and executing what we know.

THE TEACHABILITY INDEX

What is the Teachability Index?

The Teachability Index provides us with a "quick and dirty" way to measure how ready we are to learn and where we might be having some challenges. It can tell us the probability of success because much of what we get out of any learning experience has a lot to do with ourselves as a learner. And if we think about it, this is really in play any time we are trying to acquire a new skill or learn something.

The teachability index has two parts, and it is a personal assessment of:

- Your willingness to **LEARN**
- Your willingness to **CHANGE**

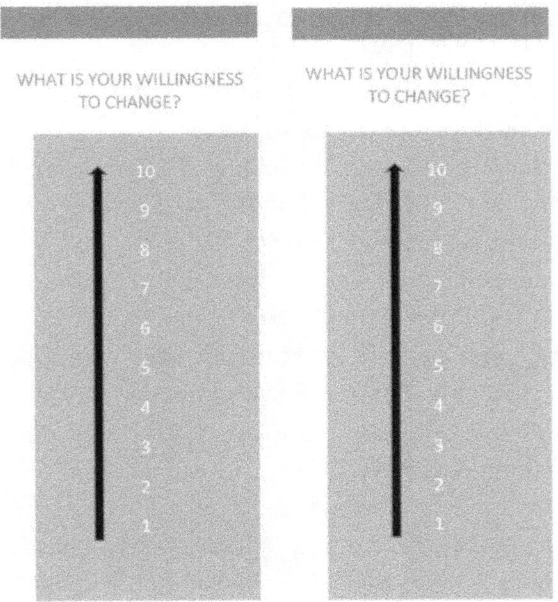

What is Your Willingness to LEARN (WTL)?

On a scale from 0 to 10, what is your willingness to learn about the subject? This can be a book, training course, exercise program, podcast, or even a meeting with a friend on a business opportunity. Quick and simple.

There are no 200 questions to answer including similar questions to determine if you were completely honest with your first response. Or filling out a dating profile and answering the question, "If you were a super-hero, who would you be?" Just one question…that's it.

We all have the desire to learn something of our interest, but it is important to consider these questions before assuming we are really willing to learn:

- Are you willing to invest money or other resources in pursuit of **knowledge**? For example, attending and paying for a seminar, taking a course, buying, and reading books, etc.
- Are you willing to invest your time for **knowledge or to learn something new**?
- What are you actually willing to give in exchange for this knowledge? Maybe it's a weekend to attend a seminar, watch a favorite TV series, golf game, etc.
- Do you like learning new things?
- Are you willing to listen to new ideas or another person's perspective? This is being open to hearing someone out before drawing quick conclusions or making decisions.

If you answered yes to all of these questions, your willingness to learn is probably pretty high. Maybe between 8 and 10. If you didn't, it is likely at the lower end of the scale, maybe between 0 and 3.

What is your Willingness to CHANGE (WTC)?

Alright, you have a strong desire to learn, but that's only half of the equation. Now, are you willing to change based on what you have learned? This is where the proverbial "rubber meets the road" or theory and idea becomes a reality.

We often prefer to keep doing what we are doing and remain where we are even if that behavior pattern is not moving us to where we want to go or achieving the results we want to achieve.

There have been many times where I have heard something or learned a new skill that I was excited to implement in my life. And then what happened? I just didn't follow through with it. I guess I wasn't willing to accept the effort required to achieve that result. Having the information to make a change and not doing anything with it is just the same as if one had not acquired that knowledge in the first place.

I work in the oil and gas industry where safety needs to be a priority, and for our company, it is a fundamental core value. Employees operate large equipment, handle hazardous chemicals, and work under potentially dangerous conditions. One small, error, a brief lapse in attention, complacency, and failure to follow established safety rules and regulations could cause extensive damage, injury to oneself or others. And unfortunately, in some cases it can prove fatal.

According to Don Brown, who writes a Safety blog, close to 90 percent of all workplace injuries are caused by the worker's own unsafe actions.[1] In addition, a majority of those incidents result from worker complacency and not following established safety rules. So an employee can be willing to learn a safety standard, BUT if they lack the willingness to change an old habit or develop a new safe one, it could prove fatal in the safety space.

To accept change is the biggest challenge to most people. The willingness to accept change is your willingness to DO what you're learning, regardless of whether it is different from the former way of doing things, or something new you are trying to implement. So if you are willing to learn, let's think about whether you are ready to accept change. This is the second question to ask yourself in the Teachability Index. Maybe these questions will help you determine this vital aspect of the model:

- Are you willing to try new things to make the **change**? For instance, a new workout routine or nutritional plan to achieve that fitness goal that's been alluding you.
- Will you try doing something new, even if it means changing your **routines, habits, patterns or preferences?** For example, waking up an hour earlier each morning to give you that extra time to exercise, journal, pray or meditate.
- How do you feel about doing something that has been **traditionally uncomfortable** for you? Are you willing and ready to tolerate some degree of discomfort? It could be something like attending a network meeting and actually walking up to people and talking to them, if this was something you previously found difficult to do. Or conversely, if you're an extrovert, it could mean attending that networking meeting, walking up to someone and actively listening to that person instead of dominating the conversation. Either way, it's moving out of your paradigm and doing something different for the sake of applying your newly acquired learning.

It's easy to see why most people may score high on their willingness to learn and lower on their willingness to accept change. Well-entrenched habits are the most difficult things to change, and most people don't have the patience necessary to develop new habits, which usually leads to failure and frustration.

How to Calculate Your Teachability Index?

Teachability Index (TI) = (WTL) x (WTC)

We can quickly determine our teachability index score by multiplying your WTL with your WTC scores. If we have 10 on both sides, you achieve 100%.

If we scored 8 on our WTL and 0 on our WTC (8 x 0 = 0), we are not very teachable or coachable since both sides should be high. If we're willing to learn but not willing to change, there will be no achievement in that particular area. Remember, don't fuss about whether it's an 8 or a 9, or 2 versus 3. The point is that it's *your* self-assessment. No one is auditing your results or asking you to submit your reasons for your choices. At the end of the day, whether your score is 0 or 30, it's still low. Alternatively, a score of 80 or 90 is pretty high, meaning you are open and ready to learn.

Martin F. enrolled in last year's Financial Literacy Program. He paid his fee, blocked off Tuesday evening for the next 2 months, and committed to completing all his assignments. After attending 3 sessions, Martin was absent for the rest of the Program.

When I followed up with him to make sure he was okay, I asked why he couldn't join us. He hummed and hawed and then said that his company was sponsoring a softball team, and his colleagues asked him to join them because they were short players. He told me he couldn't say no, so he dropped out of the Program.

If we were to initially look at Martin's Teachability Index (TI), one could say that it was somewhere in the 9-10 range for willingness to learn. He took all the initial steps to get started, paid his fees, showed up a few times and handed in those first few assignments.

Remember how we said earlier, this is where idea meets reality? I would say Martin's Willingness to Change (WTC) may also initially have been high. However, a few weeks later, the score took a "deep dive." It doesn't matter whether it was 0 or 30 percent; at the end of the day, he wasn't ready to commit to increasing his Financial Literacy for the duration of the program. At some point, he decided that softball was more important than increasing his financial knowledge.

Now, I am not judging his decision. That's a personal choice. I love playing sports, and playing on a team is a great way to have some fun and build friendships. But, do you see how we can quickly determine his **TI,** how it may even start out looking positive and then end up low by the time we need to apply the learning?

"The more one learns, the more he understands his ignorance. I am simply an ignorant man, trying to lessen his ignorance."
—Louis L'Amour

Your Attitude and the Teachability Index

As I've reflected on the Teachability Index over the years, I firmly believe that "attitude" holds an essential place in the arena of learning and being coached.

Looking at the diagram below, you will note that we have the most positive learning experiences when we are in that "student/teacher" optimal position. This doesn't necessarily mean a formal student/teacher relationship like you see in the traditional classroom. The "teacher" could be any person who knows more about the subject matter than you do. The 'teacher' or teaching/learning experience could come from a book, a movie, or a recent podcast, or any other medium.

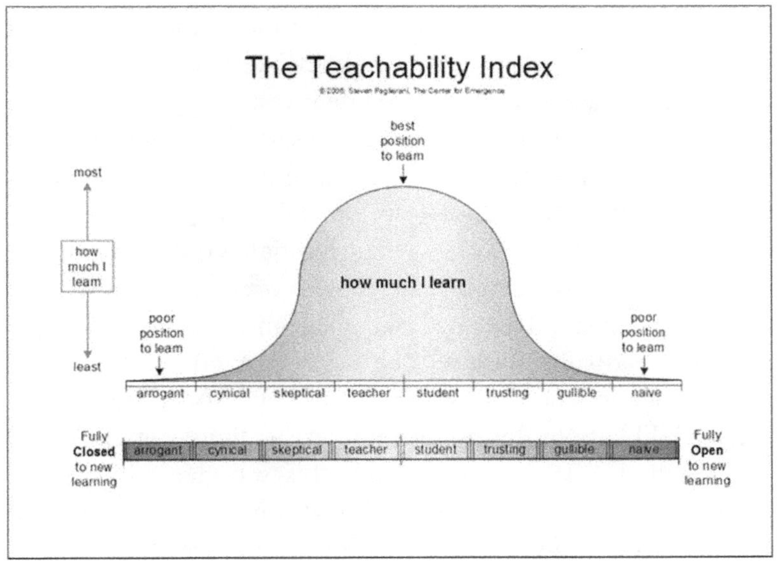

One cannot have a positive learning experience if you are at either end of the spectrum. If I am arrogant, cynical or skeptical, that attitude will impact my openness to learning and result in a low willingness to learn (WTL) score. Many people lose out on learning opportunities because they don't even give it a chance.

Similarly, if I'm on the opposite end of the scale and am naïve, gullible and trusting, and just believe and accept everything being taught, I will not learn anything. In fact, this is where I can be taken advantage of, and be at risk to make poor or bad decisions.[2]

Jay's Encounter with TI

Let me share a personal experience that demonstrates how the Teachability Index came into play. I had been out of University for about five years and started my career in the oil industry. I was interested in properties and joined a real estate investment network from another city. I would often drive five hours on the weekend to attend seminars and networking events. Over time, my investment knowledge slowly increased, and I met some successful real estate investors.

One day, I received a phone message from one of those investors. "Hi Jay! Hey listen… I have a great opportunity I want to share with you. Give me a call as soon as you can." After listening to the message, my initial thoughts were not what potential opportunity my fellow investor wanted to share with me. Instead, I became skeptical and cynical. This guy probably had some property he wanted to off load-off on a young, inexperienced investor like myself. My willingness to learn (WTL) about this opportunity was definitely low.

I waited a few days, ignoring his message to call him immediately and continued to "stew" on what this guy had "up his sleeve." Finally, as a gesture of courtesy, I called him and left a message. "Hi, this is Jay. Thank you for the opportunity, but I can't afford to buy a property right now. I just started my career and I'm taking a few courses, so I don't have time to invest. Again, thanks for thinking of me, and if another opportunity comes up at a later date, please feel free to contact me." Great job Jay! I figure I had just "dodged a bullet."

He called me back, and we got a chance to speak in person this time. And he said to me, "Jay, I respect your decision, but how did you know what the opportunity was before I even told what it was? Actually, as you know, I have several properties, and since I know you're an Accountant, I was going to propose that we make a property investment together. I would put up the money for the property, you do the accounting, and when we sell the property, we split the profits 60/40."

Shocked at the deal and knowing that I totally misread this one, I quickly said, "Wow! I didn't realize that. In that case, I would love to make that investment with you."

And this is when his following statement stung me like a

swarm of bees protecting their honeycomb. "Well, Jay, thank you, but no thanks. I'm not sure I want to work with someone who makes quick assumptions and doesn't take the time to determine the details before making a decision. I can't afford to make investments with a person who has that kind of thinking."

Ouch! That hurt! But he was right. I often think about where that partnership might have taken me. Since then, I don't use the Teachability Index (TI) as a theoretical model, but rather a quick tool that checks my attitude "at the door" and my ensures I have the right mindset to learning and opportunities.

I share this experience with my students every semester. And I follow up by telling them that if they ever have an opportunity, business idea, or an investment they want to share with me, I will make time to hear them out. I never, ever want to be so arrogant, cynical or skeptical to think that I can't learn from one of the participants.

We live in times where people can be so negative. And it seems like social media has amplified those thoughts and feelings out there. It's so refreshing when you come across some positivity. The other day, I viewed a post where a 4-year-old child played a Beethoven piece on the piano. His dog was howling in the background to the music. It was quite the achievement for such a young child, and the canine duet, to boot. The post had about 4 million likes, and then I noticed about 10,000 thumbs down. What is wrong with people? Are they that offended by this marvel, or just trolling the internet looking for an opportunity to shed negativity. Let's not be that kind of individual. There's enough arrogance and cynicism out there. Let's give everyone, including ourselves, a real opportunity to learn and be better.

There are times when we are just not in the right frame of mind to learn. We're having a bad day, we're worried about a friend or family member, or we're just plain tired. The pressures of life are real, and they can cause our attitude to shift, making us not as open or able to learn a new skill AT THAT TIME.

On a similar note, maybe you're thinking, "What does that person know?" or we hear an idea and say, "Why would that ever work?" Clearly, our Teachability Index score is low at that particular time, and there isn't a genuine desire to learn something new at that precise moment. That's okay. Don't get down on yourself and feel like you're stuck or attribute a lack of progress towards a goal as a personal failure. Just acknowledge that other things are getting in the way of advancement…like life, at that moment. Sometime later, you will be in a better mindset to learn.

The good news is that you can repeat the scoring of this index as many times as you want. I always start my classes by asking my students. "How your Teachability Index is today? Are you ready to learn? Are you anticipating some great insights tonight?"

So why is knowledge of the Teachability Index (TI) important in the pursuit of financial literacy? Financial literacy is understanding and making use of financial information so we can make sound decisions for the short and long term. If we are not open to learning new concepts, or further developing those we already know, we may be losing out on valuable teachings that would otherwise make us successful.

Summary

In this chapter, we learned that the Teachability Index is a quick way to measure how open we are to learning and accepting change. It can act as an excellent barometer to get our attitude in check to anticipate learning, and with this comes action that leads to change.

We are going to go through a lot of material in the book.

There will likely be certain things you don't agree with or maybe just not for you. That's ok! There will be other things you've heard before and maybe, it's time to make the changes that result in action. The important factor is that you are OPEN to learning and give yourself a chance to make those positive changes and help you along your financial journey.

What's Your Teachability Index (TI)?
Action Step

Go to the *Fast Track to Prosperity Workbook* and do the exercise on using the Teachability Index in everyday life.

This checklist can be accessed at
www.fasttrack2prosperity.com/bonus
Or scan this QR code with your phone camera.

4

CORE VALUES - LET'S DIG DEEP

I remember growing up in a middle-class neighborhood of immigrant families. My parents had settled in Canada from Italy, and many of my friends were first-generation Canadians. The community had the typical grocery stores, hardware, bakery, butcher shop and a musical instrument shop. The musical instrument store was one of my favorites. I would often walk around the area, but when I came to the music shop, I would always gaze at the many instruments through the window. Fascinated by the collection of woodwind, string and brass instruments, I started going in to browse around

The smell of maple, mahogany and Brazilwood would hit me the moment I walked in. I was particularly captivated by the drums as I thought it would be cool to be a drum player. Still, I realized if my dad was irritated by the sound of a tennis ball being shot by a hockey stick at the garage door, there's no way he'd put up with my constant drum pounding.

So I moved on to the pianos and keyboards. I knew a piano was outside the family's budget. However, I thought that maybe an electronic keyboard could be the instrument I could get and learn. I looked at a few models, and then my attention turned one with over twenty rhythms and more features and buttons that I could mention. The price was just over $2,000, which was a pretty penny back then, and still is today.

My next step was to talk to my dad. Delivering a spending plan that would cost the family a couple grand was not the easiest thing to do. I was only thirteen, but I had a job (more on that in the next chapter) and felt that if my dad paid for it upfront, I could pay him back over time. Well, I spoke with my parents, answering more questions than a rookie District Attorney can throw at you when making their debut on court day.

After a few weeks of thinking about it, my dad surprised me with his approval of my plan. He wanted to ensure I understood the responsibility of repaying him for the keyboard and paying for my music lessons. I agreed, and we were off to the bank for him to finance part of the purchase.

As I sat down in the bank manager's office, my dad explained why he needed the loan. Then I got to round two of questioning by the scruffy-looking man behind the big desk. I guess he just wanted to make sure I knew what I was getting into and that it wasn't just some young kid's whim. After what seemed a bit of an interrogation, he turned to my dad with a proposal. Instead of having my dad pay for the loan, he suggested I get the loan and have my father co-sign. This plan would teach me financial responsibility and help me build my credit so that by the time I reached 18 years of age, I'd be on my way to having a pretty handsome credit score.

I learned a lot about money, financing and the banking system with that loan. More importantly, my father and that bank manager were instrumental in shaping my financial core values, which we will look at in more detail over the next couple of chapters.

Do You Care about Your Personal Finances?

In the opening session of the Financial Literacy Program, I stress the importance of taking personal control, responsibility, and accountability for our finances. I am always amazed at the attitude of some individuals when it comes to money.

There's a story of a woman who said she lost her wallet with all her credit cards. When asked whether she called the credit card companies to cancel the card, she said, "Oh heck no, whoever has my cards now is spending less than my husband."

One important lesson I try to continually reinforce is:

If you don't care about your personal finances... who will?

This really comes down to our personal values around money. But, if you don't care about...

- **Being overcharged at the grocery store for an item.** *Hey man, it's only a dollar. It's no big deal. ...* **Who will?**
- **Checking your bank and credit card statement to check for any errors.** *I have no time to review statements, plus I trust the merchants and*

credit card companies. They rarely make errors… **Who will?**

- **Reducing your taxes…** *ever get a call from the CRA (Canada Revenue Agency), IRS (Internal revenue Service) or the government tax agency in your country giving you tips on how to save on taxes? I don't think so! The only call I get from the Tax Centre is those scam artists saying I owe money and call them back, so I don't get arrested … but all forgiven if I send them some funds…* **Who will?**

More importantly, with all these examples, think about what you are passing on to your children with respect to financial values. We've already seen that they're not getting solid financial training in the education system. However, as parents or influential adults in a young person's life, you are the primary educator of financial responsibility. The education system should definitely be teaching financial literacy and basics, but it cannot be put solely on the shoulders of the education system. So, if we're teaching them this attitude of letting things take their own course without actively managing our finances, they may have difficulty with money well into their adult lives.

Even if you have an accountant, financial experts or advisors managing your finances, please remember that these folks may be great professionals. Still, they are being compensated in some way for providing their services. There is nothing wrong with that, but my point is at the end of the day, they are not ultimately responsible for your finances…you are! If your investments or finances are not doing well, I guarantee you that **NONE** of these advisors will be making sure you can feed your family or top up your pension funds at retirement.

You must ask enough intelligent questions to understand how they manage your finances. This brings us back to the importance of having some financial knowledge. One doesn't have to be a financial expert, but if you're going to "farm out" the management of some of your finances, you will need to have enough knowledge to keep these folks on task in helping you achieve your financial goals.

Core Values

Our concept of money is based on our personal values. Hopefully, you'll agree with me that some of the financial decisions you make today can affect your future and that of your family for years to come. Think of some wealthy families out there. Clearly, someone in a past generation of that family made some sound financial decisions. The Waltons, Rockefellers, Kochs, and Rothschilds, to name a few. And now, for generations to come, the children, grandchildren and those yet to come are set for life. So, never underestimate the financial decisions you are making today and their effect on you and your children, *and their children.*

A person's value around money is an integral part of their being and is formed by various factors. These factors can positively or negatively impact their thinking, behavior and actions regarding finances. Some common factors are:

- Family
- Friends
- Spouse/Partner
- Personal Experiences – both positive and negative

Family

As we discussed, families can play an important part in shaping our concepts and values around money. In the personal example I shared at the beginning of the chapter, my father instilled some of his financial beliefs and practices in me at an early age. That's why it's so crucial for us to teach our children solid money principles.

Mo H., 24

We didn't have a lot growing up back in Syria and my mom and dad had to work a couple of jobs each to make sure me and my sisters could have a decent life. I guess they taught us about the value of hard work, regardless of what you do. That's always stuck with me, and what I'm trying to teach my kids now. I tell them to get a job, any job right now while you're still going to school, so they understand that there's pride and value in any type of work.

Cindy P., 29

My mom raised me and brother as a single parent. She made good money as an Emergency nurse but I'd have to say that she had a problem with debt. One time, we even came close to having our home foreclosed on. It wasn't a good time and I remember being worried about where we would live, if we lost our home. That's why to this day, other than my mortgage, I don't have any large debt and pay off my credit card balance every month.

Friends

The subject of finances is somewhat like the topic of sex. What…c'mon??? Unfortunately, finances and sex are taboo subjects in most homes. Maybe because they're uncomfortable topics to explain. We don't talk about finances early enough with kids, if at all. So what happens if they're not getting the information at home? That's right, they pick it up, whether good or bad, from their friends at the playground, on the streets, on social media, or wherever they can. The problem with this is that we don't control the message or information. It's like giving young children the remote late at night, or full access to the internet, with no parental controls. Who knows what inappropriate things they're going to see, or what spicy lyrics are going to roll off the tongue of the latest Rapper? Getting back to finances, without positive parental influence, our kids are at risk of being influenced by misinformation or by people who want to take advantage of their lack of money sense.

Influence from friends doesn't only happen while we're growing up. It can also occur as adults. You've read my story in the Introduction, so you have some sense of how easy it can occur. As a Pension and Benefits professional for a major oil and gas company, I am able to educate employees on the company's offerings. One of the most common responses I get from those who chose not to enroll in a particular benefit is, "The guys on the team told me not to get into that." Usually, that statement is followed by some myth or falsehood that is nowhere close to the truth.

Although they mean well, blindly taking a friend's or teammate's advice without doing your own homework is financially risky and foolish. I always ask the employee a few questions, <u>not to shame,</u> but hopefully to drive home a lesson. Below is how the conversation typically unfolds:

Jay: "Is the friend or teammate who gave you that advice in the same family situation as yourself?"

Employee: "No."

Jay: "Did you ask about their personal financial position? For example, are they in the same financial situation as you, or is theirs different (better/worse)?

Employee: "No, I did not ask. I don't know."

Jay: "Ok, you've received numerous employee communications over the years on this particular benefit. Is there any reason you didn't call Human Resources to ask more about it?

Employee: "No, I usually don't read that stuff we get from the company. I don't really understand it."

Jay: "Alright, no more questions. You may now step away from the stand, now. (Lol)

Ok, I don't actually say that last comment. I thought I would insert a little humor here. Who says finances can't be fun? Do you see, though, how the responses are pretty light on logic and sensibility when asking some basic questions about why they listened to their friends on a significant financial decision?

I should have ended with this question, "Now that you've lost out on that additional money you could have earned from this benefit, are any of those friends whose advice you counted on going to help put food on your table tonight or top up your pension funds for retirement?" I'm sure those friends had good intentions BUT.......

Do we see a trend here? It's only when they finally get the accurate information and knowledge that they realize they've lost out on an important and lucrative benefit that potentially amounts to tens of thousands of dollars throughout their career and into retirement. A pretty expensive mistake to carelessly count on with what may be well-intended advice from friends, without doing any due diligence on your own.

Who You Hang'n With?

Many years ago, author and motivational speaker Jim Rohn said, "You are the average of the five people you spend the most time with." The basis of that quote is that our lives are heavily influenced by our relationships. However, that's probably not totally accurate, as many of us spend most of our time with our families. I feel a more precise quote is, "You are the average of the five closest friends you spend the most time with."

When it comes to relationships, we are influenced by the people closest to us. It's only natural that hanging around with certain individuals affects our thinking, self-esteem and decisions. There is nothing wrong with that as long as we recognize this truth. Of course, we are all individuals and ultimately responsible for our choices, but the impact of our close friends cannot be discounted.

Don't get me wrong; I am not saying that we should never listen to or take advice from friends. That is what a support system is all about, and hopefully, your friends have your best interests in mind. However, if Amelie has never owned a rental property, she may not be the one to ask for insights on being a successful landlord. Or, if Sammy is deep in debt, he may not be the best guy to help you decide if you should get that extra credit card or increase your credit limit.

These factors we are reviewing can positively or negatively

affect how we make decisions about money. Let me illustrate this in the next couple of paragraphs.

Shortly after graduating from University, I met Melvin at a social function. We hit it off fairly quickly and realized we had some common interests in business and sports. We also shared some similar values in that we were both first-generation Canadians – he from Chinese parents and me from Italian. Our cultures seem to place a high value on family and a strong work ethic. Over the next ten years, we spent a lot of time together, and I would say that he was definitely one of the "five" people I hung around the most.

Melvin was a successful businessman who owned and managed over twenty properties and dozens of snack vending machines "peppered" all over the city for a thirty-something guy. More on that later. But, guess when I first started buying real estate? Yes, a few years after meeting Melvin. How about when I established a successful side business of vending machines all over the province of Alberta explicitly geared for kids of all ages? Yes, a few years after meeting Melvin.

Do you believe this is all coincidence? Well, I can tell you that it wasn't. As the friendship grew, we fed off each other. I was being mentored on business while I counselled him on accounting and other aspects of life. The point is that his thinking "rubbed off" on me, and it eventually led me to make some sound financial decisions, establishing these different streams of income while building my career as a financial professional. I would have to say that my financial net worth moved up a few "notches" while Melvin was in my closest circle of influence.

I am not advocating that you drop your current friends and only spend time with high net worth folks, so yours will increase. I'm just telling you to recognize the importance of our circle of friends and the impact and influence they can have on our thinking, behavior and core financial values.

Spouse/Partner

I'm sure most of us have heard that it's common for couples to fight and argue about money. There are numerous studies and surveys out there that support this notion. According to Cashlorette, a personal finance site, nearly half of Americans (48%) who are married or living with a partner say they argue as a couple about money.[1] Most of the fights are about spending habits, with 60% saying that one person spends too much or the other one is too stingy. The remaining 40% is divvied up between fights related to financial priorities in life, forgetting to pay a bill and being dishonest about money.

Sound familiar? It doesn't stop there; money issues could (and have) lead to divorce. Data released by the financial firm TD Ameritrade found that 41% of divorced Generation Xers and 29% of Baby Boomers say they ended their marriage due to disagreements about money.[2]

This is not surprising. It's hard enough understanding our own concepts and values around finances. Now, multiply that several fold by introducing another person into the equation. It's no wonder that a subject closely tied to our sense of well-being can profoundly impact a relationship.

Brenda,

My boyfriend, at the time brought a lot of debt into the relationship. I didn't think much about it, since we both were working and had stable jobs. A couple of years later we got married and it was an exciting time in our lives. Of course, the debt continued to increase and it caused both of us a lot of stress. He would just buy stuff and it would irritate me that we'd never talk about it as a couple. And even when we would discuss it before hand, he would just say, "I'm buying it."

That's how we got a new truck and that boat we used 3 times a summer.

It just seemed to spiral out of control. We would pay off one debt and then something else would come up. We would fight continuously about it and I became resentful towards him. It got to the point where we went to marriage counselling. After two years of that… which was just a Band-Aid solution, we decided to call it quits and divorced.

Important to understand is a person's financial values and behaviors during the dating, or "getting to know each other," stage of a relationship. This can provide many clues or "red flags" that, if not discussed and resolved in some mutually acceptable manner, will likely cause more issues later on.

Indira and Jon,

I'm a first generation Canadian and Jon was born and raised in Canada. I grew up in a family where we had to sacrifice, scrimp and save for anything. Jon was raised in a middle class family that enjoyed many of the comforts that goes with that. I kind of feel guilty spending money on expensive things or even taking family vacations but I want to make sure there's enough for our children to go on to University or College. Jon says that things are under control and we should enjoy the fruits of our labor and build experiences with our kids that they will always remember as a family. We really enjoyed the assignment Jay gave us on defining our core values. It gave Jon and me an opportunity to discuss these and come to some common ground. We didn't realize how much our different cultures could influence our personal finances.

As mentioned earlier, many newcomers to Canada are attracted to the Financial Literacy Program. Many come from different cultures worldwide, and they bring some of those financial values with them. When two individuals from different cultures come together in a relationship, sometimes financial values can clash.

As with all the other factors, the impact of a spouse or partner is not always harmful. Many times, when couples are open to learning from each other and putting aside personal agendas and ego at the door, the differences in values can actually lead to a positive experience.

Jen and Joshua,

Josh is the numbers guy in the family. My parents provided for us but I never really took an interest in finances…I just found it hard and confusing. So when I met Josh and we hit it off, I was glad to see that he knew a lot about managing money. Over the years, I've learned many things about finances from him. You know like credit card management and budgeting. He also encouraged me to take the Financial Literacy Program, which we attend together. It's been awesome. We do the assignments together and can't believe how much I've learned. The other day I was talking to my dad and he couldn't believe I gave him a "tips" on some stocks.

Personal History

Last but not least, our positive and negative experiences shape our core values. As I shared at the start of the book, my negative experience with finances brought me to the point where I had to make some critical decisions. I am glad that I didn't choose to paralyze myself in feeling like a victim and not move forward.

Life experiences are like driving a car. You can look in the rearview mirror but only to see what's left behind...the important things are ahead.

Personal events can literally shape our entire concept of money and finances. I know many people who have tried some investment or deal that didn't turn out their way and never want to take that risk again. That line of thought likely will lead to lost opportunities over time.

The other perspective from a negative experience is to learn from that event. Think of it as paying for a life lesson. I realize that some of those life lessons can be pretty expensive. But, it is better to move on, learn from those negative experiences and try not to repeat, rather than not being open to other prospective positive prospects.

Summary

Our core values and concept of money are formed by many factors, including our childhood, friends, spouses/partners, and our own personal experiences. These events can either be positive or negative, and our response to them ultimately determines how we may handle our finances in the future.

One of the most impactful aspects of finances is our

attitude towards money. If you don't care about your finances, who will? It is essential to take responsibility for our personal finances as no one else has your best interest at heart other than you.

Core Values - Let's Dig Deep: Action Step

Go to the *Fast Track to Prosperity Workbook* and do the exercise on the various factors that have affected your concept of, and core values around, finances. List those factors and write down whether they have had positive or negative impact, or both. The few examples cited from several people in this chapter may lend some ideas as you formulate your responses. This exercise will cause you to think about these elements and may better help you to understand why you think what you do about finances.

The form can be found at www.fasttrack2prosperity.com/bonus Or scan this QR code with your phone camera.

5

CORE VALUES DEUX (THAT'S TWO IN FRENCH!)

I mentioned in the last chapter that I had a job delivering newspapers at the ripe old age of thirteen. I was helping my friend's brother for a while and then got a big promotion to my own route. Today, we have instant and immediate access to information online. Some of you may not be able to relate to this, but at one time, someone would actually deliver a newspaper to your door daily so you could relax and read the world and local news, laugh at the comics or be challenged by a crossword puzzle.

Like many people, my personal history has greatly affected my perspectives on money and my financial core values. Having a newspaper route was like having a small business. You had a product that you delivered to your clients in canvas sacks over the shoulder. Boy were those heavy at the beginning of the shift! You collected money, paid invoices, and then came the expense of replacing shoes prematurely worn-out by walking dozens of kilometers a week. I learned a lot about finances, small business and, most importantly, dealing with people…my customers.

I remember one particular time; I was collecting money from delivering the newspaper. Our customers would pay for their subscription every two weeks, and I would give them their receipt: a small, perforated piece of paper the size of my thumbnail – indicating "Paid until April 20," or whatever the date was. Sometimes, people would be late paying their bills, and I would have to come up with my own money to pay for the papers until I collected the receivable.

I was fortunate that my route had a few big apartments, which meant I could deliver a lot of newspapers without having to walk from house to house. I looked forward to those apartments as they gave me a reprieve from the heat, rain, or snow, whatever the weather was, depending on the seasons here in Canada.

This one guy was behind a few payments, so I buzzed his apartment…. after a few long ringtones, he finally answered. "C'mon up," he said. I made my way up several floors and walked down the long hallway until I got to his door. Slowly knocking on the door, I waited for him to answer. Finally, I heard his footsteps as he got closer. He opened the door, we exchanged greetings and then told him I was there to collect for the delivery. He looked like I had come to ask for a blood sample and carried an axe.

He proceeded to tell me he wasn't going to pay off his small debt because a dog had chewed his newspapers several times over the last week. Feeling bad, I thought to myself, "Just my luck! Some darn dog in the apartment building eating into my profits." I didn't know what to say to the man other than, "Sorry to hear that." No sooner had the words left my mouth than a nice-sized Rottweiler came to the door behind him. He shushed him away, and now I was thinking, "Okay, the dog that ate the newspaper was yours, and now you won't pay me?"

Anyway, I left that day without payment and thought about how to handle the situation. Back then, I knew that if I had gone to my supervisor or my dad, they would have told me to just deal with it. Nowadays, the parents would likely get involved, lawyers contacted, and maybe even some counselling and therapy for the kid.

I didn't know it at the time, but you could say I was already starting to use my system. **Pause, Plan, and Prosper**. Looking back now, I'm thinking, "What a terrible thing to take advantage of a kid." I wouldn't have the heart to do that. When some child comes to my door selling cookies or chocolates, I can't buy just one box; I purchase enough to feed the whole neighborhood. If another one comes raising money to go to Disneyland, I give them an extra $50 and say, "Here, go to Europe instead."

So, back to the man with the dog… I **paused** and thought there was no way to force him to pay, so maybe I could get on his good side instead. The **plan** was to deliver his newspaper to his door, but this time I also left a can of dog food with a note saying, "I will be over on Saturday to collect the outstanding amount." That should fend off that little wolf he had as a pet.

I showed up on Saturday, and I guess my plan worked because the gentleman was so nice to me that he not only paid me what was owed but gave me a nice tip. I got to **prosper** that day and learned valuable customer service and dealing with people lessons. These experiences continued to shape my values and mindset around finances and making money.

Core Values

Our concept of money and core values are affected by various factors. Core values can be roughly defined as:

> **The foundational beliefs that a person uses to conduct themselves. They are the principle perspectives, or moral compasses, guiding a person's actions and behavior.**

In this case, it relates to finances, but our core values affect decisions that determine how we act and behave at work, with our families and friends, the community, and the environment, to name a few. While core values are integrated into all aspects of our lives, some are universally applied, and others are only pertinent to specific areas.

For our purposes, we will focus on financial core values as they subconsciously influence the financial decisions we make in life. These core values are somewhat like our personality characteristics and genetic makeup in that it's inherent in the way we conduct ourselves and behave. If asked about our personality and what makes us tick, we could probably describe it in a few words but perhaps have a more challenging time if we had to write it down. It's not something we naturally do.

When I sit down with individuals or couples for financial coaching, the first question I always ask is, "What are your financial core values?" Then, I wait for them to look at each other and display that puzzled look on their faces. It's as if to say, "What is this guy talking about, and why are we paying for this?"

In the Financial Literacy Program (FLP), one of the first assignments I get the students to do is describe their financial core values. I know many of them are probably thinking, "Teach me to pick stocks and invest in real estate. What's this about values?" After completing the assignment, one of the participants jokingly said, "I didn't realize I was taking a psychology class." Nonetheless, I believe it's one of the most basic and beneficial exercises we can do. Understanding your financial mindset and why we make certain decisions is just as important as financial knowledge.

After many years of coaching and teaching financial literacy, I've developed a list of financial core values that help guide our actions and behaviors with respect to money decisions. These elements are included here because they can lead us to make decisions that affect personal debt levels, what investments we make, how we spend and enjoy the money we earn, and how much we have at retirement. There are probably other factors that could make the list – but this wasn't part of an elaborate and costly government research study funded with taxpayer dollars – it's simply based on my personal experience with ordinary people like you and me.

Financial Core Value Listing

The following listing provides a value range for the key financial core values, and each will be described in a bit more detail.

1. Thrifty / frugal / economic vs. luxurious
2. Living for today / the present vs. saving for the future / a rainy day
3. Low-risk taker / risk-averse vs. high-risk taker
4. Purchase now vs. delayed gratification / waiting to have some or most of the required funds before buying

5. Needs (basic necessities) vs. wants (desirable, but not a necessity)
6. Passive personal financial management vs. active personal financial management
7. ThriftyLuxurious

1. Thrifty	Luxurious
A thrifty person spends their money carefully and never wastefully. They tend to be very conscientious about their spending habits. A thrifty person is not the same as being "cheap" or "stingy". This person has no problem staying at a 2 or 3-star hotel. ★ ★ ★	A luxurious person likes the finer things in life. They tend to enjoy high-quality items or services: designer brands, more expensive restaurants, etc... When on vacation, this person has to stay at 4 or 5-star hotels. ★ ★ ★ ★ ★

2. Present-day living	Future
Someone who lives for the present, enjoys life and spends based on the premise that "we don't know how long will be around, so enjoy your money today." The person who lives for today tends not to worry about saving for retirement or for a "rainy day", and likely not to have an emergency fund	This type of person saves and scrimps today because they may need money in the future. They are more likely to have an Emergency Fund. Saving for retirement is a priority and this person will often go without "today" for the sake of "tomorrow."

3. Low-risk High-risk

Low-risk	High-risk
This person does not like to take risks; they are very conservative with spending and investing. If they invest in the stock market and it goes down, they can't sleep at night. They are typically not as open to new investment opportunities or ways to make non-traditional income.	Someone who is a high-risk taker and is more liberal with their spending and investing. They believe that the higher the risk, the higher the reward. High-risk takers are more open to non-traditional investment opportunities.

4. Delayed Gratification Buy Now

Delayed Gratification	Buy Now
This type of person would rather wait until they have the money saved up or that item goes on sale before making the purchase. This does not apply to large purchases like a home or a car, where a loan might be needed.	The "buy now" individual sees something and needs to purchase right now. They don't want to wait until the prices come down on that latest technology or wait for a "sale" as it may never come. This person can be an impulse buyer.

5. Needs Wants

Needs	Wants
This individual understands that the basic necessities of life need to be handled. Food, shelter, utilities, transportation. They think twice about buying items that are not needs.	Someone in this category may recognize the difference between the two but consciously decides to spend on the "want."

6. Passive financial management	Active financial management
This person takes a passive interest in managing their personal finances. They believe their spouse/partner or financial advisor can take care of it for them. Self-development in financial literacy is not a priority.	The active person takes a special interest in their financial affairs and believes they are ultimately responsible for their finances. They seek to learn and understand financial concepts to actively manage their finances.

Main Considerations

As you consider these core values and think about where you may stand, let me clarify a few points. Wherever you place yourself on each value spectrum, there is no judgement, no right or wrong answer. It's simply a reflection of your thinking and concept around finances.

Secondly, you are not necessarily on one side or the other all the time. Sometimes, where you land on the spectrum may depend on the particular situation at that time. However, the key point is to look at where you tend to gravitate to *most of the time*.

Miranda D., 38

For the most part, I am a low-risk investor, but if the opportunity presents itself, I don't mind taking a medium risk. I was introduced to value investing by a friend a few years ago and after doing some research, I bought a couple of blue-chip, conservative company stocks and they've done very well. I'm glad I took a little more risk.

Another point is that these values don't change much over time. They're not like changing your clothes every day or selecting different food during your weekly grocery shopping trip. Values typically stay constant, guiding our decisions and behaviors. However, this doesn't mean they can't be tweaked from time to time.

Rashesh, 42

I was coaching Rashesh, and we determined that he was a very low-risk investor. He also shared that considering his excellent salary as a Sr. Engineer, he hadn't been increasing his financial net worth throughout of his career (more on Net Worth later in this Section). I asked him to identify the last five investments he considered and explain why he decided against investing in them. He named the five but could only remember why he didn't invest in three. This is what we found out and the plan forward:

When evaluating an investment and choosing not to invest, always record the reason you made that decision. Why?Most people don't do this, so how do you know if you made the right decision or not?

For the three decisions Rashesh remembered, he recalls that he just didn't want to take the risk. That's fine. He made a decision based on his analysis and his core value around risk.

We determined the current stock price for the three companies he chose not to invest in. They all increased by 14%, 27% and 38%, respectively. So, it was apparent that he did not make the best decision. Again, this was not to shame him but to see how we could correct it going forward.

Since Rashesh identified the reason for not making these suitable investments as his low-risk tolerance level, we concluded that he needed to "tweak" the level of risk he was willing to take.

Rashesh discussed this with his wife, and they both agreed that if they wanted to make some profit on investments, they would have to move to the right of the risk spectrum.

Rashesh's case was an excellent example of how our core values don't dramatically change over time. Still, if you're not getting positive or the results you're looking for, a review of them may be necessary and modifications made, as appropriate.

Finally, if you take your time and do a great job articulating your financial core values, it becomes an invaluable tool in your "financial toolbox." In fact, it is such a powerful exercise that when students complete the assignments in the Financial Literacy Program on investing, I can tell from reading their core value assignment whether they will choose to invest or not in the Case Study.

Rhea B., 26

I try to practice delayed gratification. I recognize that I can be impulsive at times and buy things before I am able to afford them-so I need to be more cautious in this area or I can get into high debt.

Growing up, our family didn't have very many financial resources, so most of the time, I feel I can differentiate fairly well between my "wants and needs." Sometimes, I do, however, buy stuff that is clearly a want. Can't resist that new version of the iPhone.

I am thrifty but not to the point of cheaper quality because at the end of the day, "you get what you pay for."

Life is precious and every day is a gift, so it's important to save for retirement but also enjoy your hard work now.

I used to be more passive in the management of my finances but I'm starting to take a more active role over the last couple of years. Reading more financial books and taking this course.

The Importance of Understanding Your Financial Core Values

Okay, so why is it important to recognize and understand your financial core values?

To begin with, understanding our financial core values helps us develop our objectives within a financial plan. In the next chapter, we will discuss how our core values relate to our financial goals.

Maria, 33, Benny, 35

Maria and Benny "hummed and hawed" about writing out their core values. I asked them to trust me, and they would clearly see the benefits.

An animated discussion about the mismatch between their financial goals and core values transpired. You see, one of their financial goals was for both to retire early, at age 58. However, their risk profile was low, Maria's core value was to "buy now," and Benny's was to enjoy the luxurious side of life.

There was clearly a "malfunction at the

junction"... a deep misalignment between their goal and financial core values.

If they wanted to retire early, that meant they would have to save and invest now to have enough funds in their retirement accounts to stop working. We reviewed the current returns on their low-risk investments, and they quickly realized a hard fact. To have the money to retire at 58, they would definitely have to move their risk level on investments from LOW to MED/HIGH.

After putting together a spending plan (more in Section 2), they could pinpoint areas of savings. These savings would come from both of them curbing their current spending habits. In turn, this excess could now go towards those medium-higher risk investments that would get them the returns needed to retire at age 58.

So, I asked the obvious question, "Maria, Benny, is your goal still to retire at 58? And, if yes, are you willing to make changes to your core values so you can reach that goal?"

After careful reflection, Maria and Benny decided on the following:

- Change retirement age for Benny to 60 and keep Maria's at age 58
- Move some of their current investments from low to medium-high risk
- Any future investments would be at a medium-high risk level
- Maria would reduce her impulse buying by waiting for a couple of days before purchasing anything over $100
- Benny would reduce his luxurious lifestyle to support investing those excess funds

When making important financial decisions, our core values act like a financial "compass," thereby keeping us on track with our financial plan. They keep us on the straight and narrow, in other words. If something we are deciding about is not aligned with our core values, then we probably shouldn't do it. With the vast volume of financial advice and literature out there directed at us, it helps us "wade through all the weeds." Our core values can remove the "noise" associated with an investment or any other 'too good to be true' venture and help protect us from being scammed.

If you can articulate your financial core values, it makes it easier to transfer and pass them to your family, friends, or any other person in your life.

Most importantly, it is helpful for you to determine if your core values align with your goals and if changes need to be made to either. Let's look at Maria and Benny's experience.

Maria and Benny were glad that I persisted in getting them to write out their financial core values. Now, do you see the benefit of determining if your core values are aligned with your financial goals? Whether Maria and Benny reach their goal of early retirement is still yet to be determined, but I would have to say they have a better chance of achieving it now than they did before the review. Without this assessment, they would have gone on their merry way, investing in low-return investments and spending money that could have been used to achieve their financial goal. And then, getting close to the age of 58 and realizing they're nowhere close to being able to retire.

Again, there was nothing wrong with any of their core values. However, if they wanted to reach their financial goal, something had to change. It's best for them to know sooner and make any necessary adjustments to either a core value or a goal rather than be disappointed in the end.

What Understanding Your Core Values is NOT

This is not an exercise in getting everyone to be the same. As described earlier, we are all different and come with a wide range of experiences and ideas that shape our own core values. How you rate your core values may be different than mine and there's nothing wrong with that.

Cliff S., 46

I have a medium-risk tolerance for most of my investments but will use a small portion of my investments (maybe 5-10%) for higher risk opportunities as they become available.

I'm what you would describe as the perfect consumer… advertising and marketing affects what I buy and I often realize later that what I've purchased is more of a "want" than a "need."

I believe there needs to be a good balance between living for today and saving for the future. After all, having a lot of money in the bank is useless if you're not around to enjoy it.

I am definitely an active manager of my finances. I want to know where my money is going and how my investments are performing. I'm still working on getting my budget system down and believe in lifelong learning for my financial knowledge. Awesome

---

Summary

The concept of core values runs deep, especially related to finances. These are the foundational beliefs we use to conduct ourselves and guide our financial actions and behavior. I have identified six of the most common financial core values, and they get at the heart of how we approach spending and the management of our money.

Most people have never identified or written down their core values, but it's an invaluable exercise. When identifying your core values, there isn't a "right" or "wrong" answer – it's all about your personal beliefs and principles.

Core Values Deux (That's Two in French!): Action Steps

Go to the *Fast Track to Prosperity Workbook* and do the exercise on core values. From the list of core values, identify which one generally applies to you and then write out and explain why you made that selection. Look to some of the other examples of individuals provided in this chapter as a guide.

The core values form can be found at
www.fasttrack2prosperity.com/bonus
Or scan this QR code with your phone camera.

6

GOALS WITH HOLES

After the goal-setting workshop, Johnny's life was never the same

"Anybody with a definite purpose and with full faith in his or her ability to realize that purpose, cannot be permanently defeated."
—Napoleon Hill

After completing the core values exercise during my coaching and the Financial Literacy Program sessions, I ask the next question, "What are your financial goals?" The response for most folks comes a little easier than the Core Value discussion. Usually, they're not rolling their eyes as much. And I get some fairly common ones:

- Buy a home
- Have a lot of money
- Invest in stocks
- Retire early
- Buy a new car
- Invest in a rental property
- Save for my children's education
- Open a small business

I'm not sure what percentage of people actually write out their goals. Some individuals say they have goals, but they're just in their heads. Maybe that's the case, but I know that very few of my friends physically write out their financial goals.

I always listen to the language people use when describing their goals. "I hope to......" "We want to...." "I'd like to...." Like a child reluctantly asking a parent for that last cookie in the cookie jar, it's almost like they're asking me for permission or acceptance of their goals.

In the book Magic Ladder to Success, Napoleon Hill, one of the most accomplished self-development authors of our time, addresses the importance of having a definite goal. He explains how he studied more than 20,000 people from all walks of life during his journalistic and writing career. He found that 95% of them were barely existing or not doing well. The other 5% he considered successful, in that they were meeting all their needs and saving money for the sake of ultimate financial independence.[1]

The noteworthy point of this discovery was that the 5% had a definite purpose and a plan for attaining that purpose. That means that those who knew what they wanted and had a plan for getting it were succeeding. Those who didn't end up in that 95% category.

Like core values, we are not accustomed to really thinking about financial goals, let alone writing them out. We tend to think of them as wishes rather than definite aims or objectives. There is a significant difference between a wish and a specific goal accompanied by a plan. I can wish to win that huge lottery and daydream about what I would do with that jackpot… retire and travel the world… help my family and friends… give to causes I care about…and so on, and so on. Oh, to dream!

But, deep down, I know the chances of me winning the lottery are about the same as me playing professional basketball in the NBA this year: next to nil. I'm a numbers guy. I know the probability, and it's not in my favor. My only plan to win involves at least buying one ticket, and that's it. It's out of my control, and there's nothing more I can do to ensure I win.

In contrast to a wish, I can have a definite goal to buy a home, and more importantly, implement a plan to increase my chance of success. I may need to save $500 a month for 5 years to have enough for a down payment. Between the fourth and the fifth year, I will start looking at homes in my neighborhood. I may want to use the services of a real estate agent to help me make that purchase. I may also want to go to the bank and get a pre-approval on the mortgage to know my limit when I go home shopping. And, of course, along the way, I can monitor that goal and see if I'm on track. If not, I will make the necessary adjustments to ensure I can successfully attain my goal.

In other words, if I only dream of owning a small business without any concrete plans, it's like the lottery wish above. However, if I have an intense desire to start a business, then that requires a plan and check points along the way. This entails looking for a location, registering my company, researching what my prospective clients would want, which countries I will source my purchases from, etc.

Along the way to that final goal of opening my store, there will possibly be some setbacks and challenges that will cause me to adjust my plan. I will need to be prepared for these. However, nothing will stop me if I have a strong and passionate desire to accomplish my goal. See the difference?

I spend time ensuring the understanding between focusing on objectives versus relying on wishes because it is such an essential concept of the financial journey. But, first, let's clarify some concepts.

How They Come Together - Goals, Mission and Core Values

Goals

All serious organizations begin the year with goals. These can be defined as specific objectives or targets. For instance, the oil and gas company I work for aims to produce 125 million barrels of oil this year. A non-profit community group has a goal of serving 2,000 meals a month. The Health Department of the Canadian government aims to vaccinate 80% of the population.

Mission

Goals typically stem from an organization's mission or reason for existence. The oil and gas company's mission is to produce oil reliably, profitably and in an environmentally responsible manner. For the non-profit, it may be to provide basic necessities to those in need in the community. And for the government, it's to help Canadians maintain and improve their health.

Core Values

We have spent the last two chapters talking about personal core values. But if we looked at the oil and gas company's core values, they may be focused on using the leading technology to produce their products. Perhaps they will work with Indigenous stakeholders in the region to ensure they are consulted on major initiatives, environmental protections, and ways these groups can participate in the economic benefits of the partnership. With respect to the employees, they may articulate how they value diversity and inclusion, or career opportunities, in their workforce.

The core values for the non-profit may center on the way they want to be of service to the community, ways to ensure they treat every person with dignity and respect and being a good steward of the resources provided to them to carry out their mission.

For the Health Department, it could look like taking pride in what they do, building a workplace community and caring for the people of Canada.

It's easy to see the interrelationship between these three concepts. Although we aren't going to look at developing a personal mission statement in this book, some people may do this as it helps them streamline what they want to achieve in life. Here, I want to stress the importance of developing personal financial goals.

What Do You Want Out of Life Financially?

Begin with the End Goal in Mind

To get the ball rolling on this part, I ask people to think about two types of categories:

1. Lifestyle Goals – What do you want to do and why?

- What do you aspire for yourself and your family?
- What excites you; brings you joy?
  - Like the core values, this is a personal choice. There is no right or wrong answer. It's really about what kind of life you and your family want to live.
  - No judgment; NO shame…. It's you.
- How do you want to live your life now?
- Here are some questions that might get you thinking about what kind of lifestyle you want as it will ultimately determine your financial goals:
  - Do you want to rent vs. own a home?
  - What size of a house do you want?
  - Do you want to travel or take family vacations? If yes, where do you want to travel? Is it within your own location, country, or international travel?
  - What hobbies or activities do you and your family like to do? Do you want to enroll your kids in other activities such as sports, dance, music lessons, etc.?

- Do you prefer eating at home? Or do you enjoy eating at restaurants? How often would you like to do so if you enjoy eating out?
- What about other entertainment activities such as theatre, concerts, cultural events?
- Do you want to financially support charitable causes?
- What about your children's education?
- Others?

▸ And in retirement?

- At what age do you want to retire? If you have a spouse/partner, will you want to retire at the same time?
- In your retirement, where would you like to live? Will you live somewhere else part of the year?
- Do you want to travel once you retire? If so, how much travel do you envision doing?
- What hobbies will you have in retirement?
- Others?

2. Financial Goals

Based on the lifestyle you've identified above, we can start thinking about your financial goals that will allow you to live the life you want NOW and in RETIREMENT.

S.M.A.R.T Goals But With A Twist

To make it easier to classify your goals, I tend to group them into three different time frames. Again, there is no science to this. You can change the length to fit your own personal preferences. I say this just because one of my students wanted to know why I chose two years for the outer limit of the short-term goal instead of one. After 20 minutes of discussion, I'm sure he thought he was on a national debating stage. I told him that he could make the limits whatever he desired. The terms I suggest (as guidelines) are:

- Short-term: 6 months – 2 years
- Medium-term: 3 – 5 years
- Long-term: more than 5 years

We use a goal-setting process called S.M.A.R.T goals in the company where I work. It's one way to approach it, but I must declare upfront that it doesn't really consider all the important aspects for me.

Many organizations, educators and trainers use the S.M.A.R.T process to set their goals.

This method is meant to help people reach their goals by ensuring they are:

- **S**pecific
- **M**easurable
- **A**ttainable/Achievable
- **R**elevant
- **T**ime-bound

For instance, as stated above, most people create very general goals whether they are lifestyle or financial goals. Here's an example of what I mean.

General Goal: I want to save enough money for my children's education.

S.M.A.R.T Goal: Over the next 15 years**,** we will save $200/month for each of our two children; in a medium risk investment to provide a lump sum amount of $35,000 each for Linda and Jason that can be used for their post-secondary education.

The general goal is pretty vague and uninspiring. How much is enough money, who's it for, where is the money being invested and for how long? This is one of those good-intentioned goals that usually ends up being side-tracked, especially if not disciplined enough to set the money aside. Maybe if there's money left at the end of the month, it goes towards the children's education, if not, maybe next month. Do you see how this type of goal is just "too loose" and perhaps not the best option? Who knows whether there will be enough money for those kids to go to college or for any other post-secondary institution? Good luck, Linda and Jason. You may have to get a side job before attending or finishing your schooling.

On the other hand, the S.M.A.R.T goal is very specific. We know precisely the amount being invested and in which type of investment. It's measurable. We know at the end of every month, and at the end of the 15 years, whether the goal was achieved or not. It's obviously relevant as it is for the children's education. Finally, it has a time frame of 15 years. The probability of accomplishing this goal is much higher than the general goal in the example above.

S.M.A.R.T. Goals that are Smarter

So, what's the problem with the S.M.A.R.T goal-setting framework? There is nothing wrong with this framework. It's widely used in organizations for employee goal-setting. However, even with an excellent goal-setting method, it doesn't guarantee successfully achieving goal attainment. Individuals may start off with good intentions and a well-documented S.M.A.R.T. goal, but at some point, there's a setback, challenge, or life just gets in the way; and the goal is abandoned.

Without evaluating goals on a regular frequency and adjusting as needed, goal attainment may not be entirely successful. This is where the S.M.A.R.T.E.R goal-setting framework emerges. Adding two additional steps: Evaluate and Re-adjust. Evaluating goals will help maintain focus on your goals and enable you to 'Re-adjust' to stay on track.

But wait! There's more…There are still two essential elements to successfully staying on track to achieve goals. I'll get to that in a minute. Remember when we discussed the lifestyle goals above? It really was about **WHAT** you want to do and **WHY?** The first element is *intent* or *purpose*. What is the reason you want that lifestyle goal? Why does it excite you? Why are you passionate about it?

In the examples below, you can tell from Joan and Bert's lifestyle goals that taking family vacations and starting a homeless shelter in the community is the fire that ignites them. These are the goals that bring them joy and satisfaction.

Bert C., 45

I've been very blessed to live in this city and it has been good to me and my family both personally and financially. Unfortunately, the number of men and women living on the streets here have increased over the years. We want to give back to this community and we plan to retire here and support where we can. Many church groups provide meals and temporary housing for those in need, however, I believe the city is ready for a larger homeless shelter. I want to offer my time, resources and contacts in the community to see if we can make this happen.

Joan J., 27

As a child, I always remember our family vacations. We would go to the lake every weekend during the summer and my sister and my cousins and myself would go swimming, hiking and canoeing for hours. That gave me the best memories, so I want to do the same for our children. We want to have at least one family vacation a year while the girls are young because I know once they start getting older it will be harder to do. I know that by making a few small changes to our spending, we can make these family vacations a reality.

The American Society of Training and Development found that people are 65 percent likely to meet a goal after committing to another person. Their chances of success increase to 95 percent when they build in ongoing meetings with their partners to check in on their progress.[2] Therefore, the second element not as explicit in the S.M.A.R.T model is *accountability*.

Accountability is critical. It involves having both the ability and the willingness to give an honest account of your actions, behavior and progress to someone else who can help you in your journey to achieve your goal. An accountability partner or coach is one of the most effective ways to stay on track and be held accountable to your SMARTER goals. Many people use an accountability partner for health programs, education or professional purposes. In the financial space, this individual could be:

- Your partner/spouse, especially if these goals have been developed as a family unit. It's also a way to keep each other accountable.

- Friend with some level of financial literacy. This person should be able to challenge you on your actions, behaviors and progress.
- Financial advisor – this person should have the financial expertise and your best interests in mind.

While it's important to always hold ourselves personally accountable, it's also important and helpful to be accountable to others. It's one thing to give up on a goal and deal with it on a personal level but if we fail and it's public, well, that's a different story. When we know that someone will ask us how we're progressing towards a goal, there is more incentive to accomplish it. This could mean the difference between giving up and being successful for many individuals.

Developing Goals 2.0: S.I.T.A.M.A.

S.I.T.A.M.A. This is my acronym for a new and improved way to develop goals. And yes, I know it's not a word. I'm sure I won't be using it the next time I play scrabble. But it does incorporate many of the previous elements and the additional intentional and accountability features.

Specific: I believe this is one of the most critical aspects of developing goals. In my experience, creating goals that are too general is the most common oversight of many of my students and clients. I tell the students when returning this assignment that the "red" ink on the page is the color of love and intended to help them improve. It's not uncommon for many of them to redo this exercise because we're not used to writing these goals in specific terms. Stating precisely what you want to accomplish is key.

Intentional: It all begins with the intent – the WHY. This is what makes your goal personal and connected only to you. While two individuals may have the exact wording for their goal, what makes up that goal is individual to that person and comprises the experiences, intentions, motivation, and dreams. In this way, like a fingerprint, no two personal goals are identical and the "Why" often becomes your greatest motivator for accomplishing that goal.

Timeframe: A goal without a timeframe is like a broken record; it goes on and on, with no end in sight. In this case, it could well mean that we never finish what we started. Open-ended goals can also give us an excuse to procrastinate and put it off "to another day." In my time, I've had many goals, "put off" to another day that never happened. If we are bound by a time, it can give us that sense of urgency required to get to the finish line.

Achievable: I believe all goals should be achievable. If a company, at the plant's full capacity, typically produces one million chocolate bars a month (I want to work there), it's reasonable to have a goal with a stretch target of a few percent above that. But if the manager states their goal next month is to produce 2 million bars that is totally unrealistic and not achievable since they're already producing at full capacity. It's no different with financial goals. Sometimes, I'll read a goal and think, this is unrealistic, or the person didn't entirely think this through.

Abby, 34

Abby created a goal that stated she wanted to purchase two rental properties in a particular city by 2025. She said she would meet this goal by saving $500/ month for the respective down payments. I applauded her positive attitude and desire to purchase some assets that could build longer-term wealth; however, the goal was unrealistic. Unless she was planning to buy the properties with some other partners, there was no way she could have enough money for one property, let

> alone two. After some brief consulting, we discussed her options. Either she had to dramatically increase the amount she was saving every month, or she would have to move the date out by several years. She decided the latter.

When our targets are too unrealistic or unachievable, in most cases, failure is inevitable. And when we fail, it could affect our psyche and prevent us from trying again. This can be avoided, if we just ensure that our goals are realistic and achievable.

Measurable: Management thinker Peter Drucker is quoted as saying "If you can't measure it, you can't improve it." What he means is that you can't know whether you are successful unless success is defined and tracked. If you have a clearly established metric for success, you can quantify progress and adjust your process to produce the desired outcome. Without it, you're stuck in a constant state of guessing.[3]

"If you can't measure it, you can't improve it."
—Peter Drucker

At the end of the time frame established in your goal, you should be able to measure whether you've achieved the goal or not.

Accountability: As we discussed earlier, having accountability tied to the goal process is integral and can make a big difference in achieving success. It is definitely worthwhile finding an accountability partner to help you along the way.

Your Daily Routine...Read and Write Them Out

There you have it. Use S.I.T.A.M.A in the goal-setting process, and you will be on the road to experiencing success. A couple of final points on this subject. When writing out your goals, use words that suggest that you will, or have already accomplished them. Instead of saying, "I want to have $2,000 in an emergency fund," claim it and say, "I HAVE or I WILL HAVE $2,000 in an emergency fund."

Secondly, after writing out your goals, don't just leave them in your notebook and forget about them. Make it a habit to read your goals every day. Bring them into your subconscious to the point where they become automatic. I'm not into the belief that if you just think hard about something, it will somehow materialize out of thin air. However, I believe that the more you own your goals, think upon them and believe you can and have achieved them, opportunities will come your way.

Our minds are so influential that when we consistently imagine and visualize our goals and combine this with belief (and an actionable plan), we WILL achieve them. The subconscious picks up every subtle message we feed it, which is why it is important to think and focus on the positive.

I'm not sure if this has happened to you, but I remember when I bought my first car. It was one of my goals for a long time, and I had been thinking about every aspect of it. I had the model, year, and color all picked out. I thought long and hard about the options and how nice it would feel to drive my very own vehicle. I finally got that car, and suddenly, it seemed like I saw my car everywhere. It was around town, on the freeway, on my way to work and on several road trips I took. Why was that? Did the Universe suddenly play a trick on me and decide to flood the area with the exact car I now owned, just because Jay had that car? Of course not. What happened was my subconscious was more in tune with my type of vehicle, so I saw it more often.

The same happens with our goals. The more we think and ponder upon them, the more opportunities to accomplish them will appear.

Sabrina, 34

> I found the assignment we did on core values and writing out our goals very beneficial. I did get into the habit of reading them every day during the course. It kind of felt funny at first, just reading them out… my kids thought I had lost it. I had always wanted to have my own home cleaning business but didn't know how I would get it started as it takes some money upfront. A couple of months after the course, while waiting for a prescription at the pharmacy, I was browsing through the magazine rack. I came across one on franchises and bought it. As I read it, I saw that there were a few Custodial franchise opportunities. I did some further research and although I didn't sign on with any of them, the information I got while doing this gave me a lot of ideas on how to start. It's now has been a couple of years since owning my cleaning business and it's doing better and better every year.

Coincidence that she just came across a resource that helped her start her dream business? Maybe, and we could probably debate that for a while, but Sabrina strongly feels that she was "in tune" with her goals and the opportunities ultimately presented themselves.

I recently read an article in a financial magazine that focused on the habits of some successful people. A reporter asked Daymond John, one of ABC's Shark Tank hosts and a very wealthy businessman, what he does on a daily basis. "Each morning, write out your goals: goals for today, for the year, for five years and for 10 years. And then read them out loud. Don't just read it so you say it. Read it so you can hear it. Change your daily goals as needed, but keep the others, long-term goals. Add to them if needed. But read them. Participate in your process." [4]

So, if an individual whose worth about $500M at the time of this writing shares a habit about his goal-setting process, should we listen? Is there something we can learn from his daily ritual and the importance he places on it?

Every so often, there's some article that comes out stating that "goals are a waste of time" or "they serve no purpose in today's environment." These authors are usually looking for their few minutes of fame, and then they disappear and move on to some other subject matter they are trying to discredit. Now, I am all for change and improvement, but purposeful thinking and goal setting have been around for thousands of years. They're not going anywhere.

I've never been to see the Great Pyramids in Egypt, but it's on my bucket list of places to visit. I've always marveled at its architecture, majesty and construction. Does anyone for a second think that at some time, thousands of workers just showed up in desert heat and started moving stones, and then they just magically formed a shape we now call a pyramid?

Or is it more plausible that someone or some group of people started thinking about a place to bury the Pharaohs? And then, probably for years, continued to develop the thought around it. They probably set some goals with committed actions and timelines around this extraordinary construction project. I'm sure they encountered numerous obstacles and setbacks along the way, but I can only marvel at how much planning and execution went into this monumental undertaking. I'd hate to be the Project Manager on that job!

Pass It On

Creating goals is essential for developing financial success, and it's one of those habits that your children will be forever grateful to you for passing on to them. When my son turned sixteen, I thought, okay, it's time for this kid to learn a bit about goals. So, I took him through a bit of background around goal setting. I then asked him what his goals were. He was in grade 11 at the time, and he looked at me like I had three heads, and kind of hummed and hawed. Throwing him a lifeline, I asked him if he planned on finishing high school." He goes, "Yeah, of course." I told him to write that down.

He says he was going to finish high school anyway, so why write it down? I asked him a simple question, "is that important to you, and is it something you want to finish in the next year?' He answered yes. We added getting his driver's license, learning guitar, learning a third language – Italian - and getting a summer job. The final and high-priority goal was determining what he wanted to study after finishing high school. In a matter of about half an hour, we had about five or six goals mapped out for him. These were all short-term, and we didn't work on his medium and long-term goals in that session, but we'll get to that later.

I graciously volunteered to be his accountability partner. He viewed it more as Dad, extending his reach over his life and getting more involved in the progress of his newfound goals. Teenagers. Well, this was a good start for him. And even though I did very little checking in with him, I noticed that he had posted his goals on a bulletin board above his desk. In less than a year, he got that summer job that also extended into his school year, kept learning guitar and Italian and completed his driving school lessons. Most importantly, he finally decided what he wanted to study, and was accepted at the two Universities he applied to.

Coincidental? Maybe. But I'm thinking he probably

learned an important lesson in goal setting that he can take into adulthood.

If most adults do not write out their goals, what percentage of high school students do you think does? It's probably even lower. This is not to say there aren't driven and determined students out there. All you have to do is read some of the accomplishments of these young kids, and you know they are ambitious and motivated to succeed. But, just like adults who never have goals but achieve success, maybe if they did write down their goals, they could achieve them faster or even surpass their expectations for themselves.

Finally, never underestimate the opportunity we have to influence our children by our coaching, teaching and example around personal finances.

So Will It Work?

Dr. Matthews, a professor at the Dominican University of California, conducted a study on how goal achievement in the workplace is influenced by writing goals, committing to goal-directed actions, and accountability for those actions. Dr. Matthews found that more than 70 percent of the participants who wrote out their goals with actionable commitments and sent weekly updates to a friend reported successful goal achievement, compared to 35 percent of those who kept their goals to themselves, without writing them down.[5]

I was at a conference several years ago where the speaker spoke about the importance of self-development. He went on to say that the average person spends more money on the outside of their head (things like hair styling, hair products and grooming) than inside of their head. Of course, everybody was looking at each other and laughing, but I had to admit, it was probably true.

His comments, although lighthearted and witty, stuck with me. At the time, I did a quick calculation; haircuts once a month, shaving razor, lotion, and all that man stuff, totaled about six to seven hundred dollars a year on hair and face grooming. Disappointingly, there were many years that I did not pass that simple self-check. From that time on, I vowed to budget at least as much on the inside as the outside. I ensured that I included self-development objectives when putting together my goals. I encourage my students to do the same, as this can be an integral part of developing and increasing financial knowledge.

As we approach the end of this long chapter; thanks for sticking with me on this, here a few examples of goals using the S.I.T.A.M.A. method:

Brandy H, 28

Specific, Timeframe, Measurable, Achievable: I will pay off the remaining $4,500 student loan my parents took out for me while attending Technical school by December, 2021.

Intentional: In doing this, it will bring me closer to being debt free by the age of 30 and I don't want to have this debt "hanging" over me going forward.

Accountability: My parents

Nelly, 42, and Simeon S., 45

Specific, Timeframe, Measurable, and Achievable: We will have $10,000 in our investment account by June, 2022 by investing $500/month. The investment will be in a maximum of 10 different stocks and across 3 different industries.

Intentional: We've always wanted to manage our investments and learning how to pick stocks is a major step to doing that. We will feel a lot more comfortable making these choices on our own rather than relying on financial advisor and paying high management fees.

Accountability: With each other every time we review our monthly finances and investment account quarterly.

Dale P., 47

Specific, Timeframe, Measurable, and Achievable: I will complete Levels 1 and 2 of the Financial Literacy Program (FLP) by the end of 2021. I will also read one self-development or financial book every 2 months.

Intentional: I have the financial know-how and can make good financial decisions for me and my family. I can understand the business news and how it affects me.

Accountability: My wife Emily

Summary

In this chapter, we learned about the importance of having goals. Most people do not have explicit goals, or at the very least, never write them down. If they do write them down, they are often so general, rendering the exercise ineffective.

An excellent model to use when writing out goals is the S.M.A.R.T. method. We also added two essential elements to the model, intention, and accountability. The upgraded template is S.I.T.A.M.A.

Readers are encouraged to read their goals every day, so they become engrained in their minds and subconscious. Many successful people go the extra step and write out their goals daily to further crystalize them in their minds.

Individuals who write out their goals, commit to actions and have someone they're accountable to, are more likely to reach their goals than those where this is absent.

Finally, don't be hesitant to teach your children about the importance of developing goals and then help them to progress those goals to completion. They will be forever grateful to you for this knowledge.

Goals with Holes: Action Steps

Now it's your turn. Go to the *Fast Track to Prosperity Workbook* and do the exercise on establishing your goals. Start the goal writing process by identifying your lifestyle goals. This is based on what you want and why. Then proceed to writing out your financial/ self-development goals. Use the S.I.T.A.M.A. format in establishing these goals.

The goals spreadsheet can be accessed at www.fasttrack2prosperity.com/bonus Or scan this QR code with your phone camera.

Access Your Workbook
SCAN HERE
TO GET YOUR
WORKBOOK
POINT YOUR PHONE
CAMERA HERE
Tap The Link
WARNING: DO NOT MOVE FORWARD BEFORE SCANNING

7

YOU'RE WORTH A LOT MORE THAN YOU THINK

One of the last topics I want to review in this first phase of "Pause" is the subject of net worth. After developing your financial goals and understanding the role your core values play in reaching those goals, it's important to know the current state of your financial position.

Think of your net worth as a current snapshot of your financial health. In more simple terms:

ASSETS – Liabilities = Net Worth

It compares what you OWN (your assets) to what you OWE (your liabilities)

When I talk about net worth, I refer to financial net worth. A student came up to me one day after class and said, "Finances aren't the only thing that makes up a person's worth, you know?" And I totally agree. Every person on this earth is special, unique and valuable as a human being. Since we were in a financial literacy class, I thought we were simply referring to finances. Hence, I wanted to make that point clear upfront.

So why is it important to determine your net worth?

1. It helps establish your short-term and long-term financial goals. After calculating your net worth, you may want to go back to your financial goals, make some adjustments, or even add one or two.
2. It reveals your current financial status. One can't do effective planning without knowing what resources are available to use. If I want to go out and buy a house, or rental property, I need to know how much funds I have to work with. This will tell me what price range I can afford, what mortgage I may require and other aspects of purchasing real estate.

Before we get into the calculations, let's review some basic standard terms. A net worth statement is the listing of assets and liabilities. When you subtract your liabilities from your assets, the balancing figure is your net worth.

Companies prepare a similar calculation, called a Balance Sheet or Statement of Financial Position. For small businesses, assets less liabilities is called owner's equity. And for corporations, the same calculation is called shareholder's equity, as the value of the company is owned by the shareholders who have invested in it.

Personal vs Business Accounting

Personal accounting is similar to accounting for businesses, except for a few differences.

1. Personal Use. First of all, no one outside of you and your family needs to see the results. It's up to you if you want to share it with anyone like a financial advisor, banker, or the like.

When a company prepares a financial statement, if they are a publically traded company (a company where you can buy shares in the stock market), the statements must be made public and available for current and potential investors to see.

2. Lenders will use your net worth statement. If you go to a bank, call or apply online for a loan or mortgage, the first thing the bank will do is prepare a quick net worth statement for you. To determine your net worth, they will ask what you own (home, car, investments, etc.) and how much you owe on any of those. However, they will leave certain assets, such as household items, out of the calculation.

3. Not a pure accounting exercise. The third difference is that you don't need to follow generally accepted accounting principles (GAAP) in determining your net worth. We're not trying to account for every dollar. It is simply a reasonable estimate of what you own and what you owe.

Definition:

GAAP – are a collection of commonly followed accounting rules and standards for financial reporting.

Importance of the Net Worth Statement

As discussed, the net worth statement is an essential part of understanding your current financial position. Here are the main reasons:

1. Progress towards financial goals: Your net worth statement provides a benchmark or measure of progress in meeting your personal or your family's goals. After completing this exercise, you may want to go back to your financial goals and create a goal to increase your net worth by a certain number or percentage. For example, "I will increase my net worth by $10,000 this year, or 10%." This way, you can use it as a metric or benchmark in your goals.

When I first started using net worth as a goal, I would look forward to calculating this measure every couple of months and get excited to see my personal equity increase. I knew that I was either increasing an asset or decreasing a liability, which increased my net worth.

2. A listing and valuation of your assets and liabilities. This exercise also provides you with a listing and the current valuation of the assets and corresponding liabilities you have to manage. The assets could be physical, like a car or home, or be monetary, like $10,000 in an investment account. I'm always amazed how many people do not know how much they OWN, or just as important, how much they OWE. Many individuals have never created a listing and valuation of their assets, or it's quickly prepared at the bank when applying for a loan. It may not be an accurate picture of their true financial position.

Here's a simple example of the Jones family's net worth statement. The total assets less the total liabilities give us the balancing figure, which is the net worth of $153,000. If the Jones sold all their assets for cash and paid out all the liabilities, they would have about $153,000 in cash.

The Jones Net worth Statement 31-Dec-21				
Cash	2,000		Credit Card	1,500
Car	20,000		Utilities	500
House	400,000		Car Loan	10,000
Furniture	8,000		Mortgage	275,000
Stocks	10,000		Total Liabilities	287,000
			Net worth	153,000
Total Assets	440,000			440,000

What to Include and Determining the Values

We see from the Jones example that their net worth could have been significantly different depending on what assets and liabilities they included in their calculation. Should they have included furniture? They also have a pack of pens; should that have been considered? How about the kid's knapsack?

More importantly, the dollar value the Jones family has placed on the assets and liabilities could have made a significant difference to the net worth calculation. This is a vital part of the exercise because they could have over-valued the assets and undervalued the liabilities, or vice versa. Both situations would have garnered an incorrect net worth result. Again, if it's off by a bit, not a problem, but if the values used are significant, it could be an issue. They may have fewer resources at their disposal to invest or could impact important plans, like when to retire based on inaccurate data.

Assets to Include:

Financial Assets

These are assets that you will currently use or are part of what you will consume at a later time (i.e. retirement). For instance, cash in your bank account can be used for groceries and paying off your bills. In other words, your current consumption.

You may also have put money away for investments, retirement or an emergency fund. These are financial assets that can be used for future use.

Personal Use Assets

These are assets that are used on a daily basis. They don't yield income, but they provide us with vital consumption. Think about items in your home like plates, linen and clothes. These articles all cost money, right? Unfortunately, individuals who may have lost personal use assets in a fire or flood know very well that the financial cost to replace them can be substantial.

Luxury Assets

Although these assets are for personal use, they are usually considered marginal to the family's needs and wants. However, luxury assets can provide high value if liquidated. For instance, jewelry, collections, or art are common examples.

Here is an example of assets in the three different categories:

Financial Assets	Personal Use Assets	Luxury Assets
• Cash on hand • Registered Pension Plans (RRSP's in Canada; 401K's in USA) • Company Pension Plans • Investments (stocks, bonds, mutual funds, ETF's Exchange Traded Funds, etc.) • Precious metals (Gold, silver), gemstones • Real Estate (personal home) • Rental Properties	• Vehicle(s) • Furniture • Clothing • Household Supplies • Sporting Equipment (hockey gear) • Maintenance equipment (lawnmower, snow blower) • Electronic items (cellphones, computers)	• Jewellery • Vacation Property • Collections (stamps, coins, dolls, sports cards, etc.)

Human Capital In or Out?

Human capital is something I often get asked about by students when they are considering what to add as assets and whether it should be included. So, it's important to know what it is first.

Human capital is the economic value of a person's abilities and qualities that can influence their earning power.

Human capital should not be valued as part of the net worth calculation. Its estimation is difficult to calculate and may seriously skew a financial analysis. For instance, if someone made $50,000 per year, that would add up to $1 million over 20 years (not taking into account inflation or potential wage increases). We wouldn't put that one million in our asset column. First, there is no guarantee that the person will have that job for 20 years, and the other reason is that the salary has yet to be realized. This means that the cash is not yet in their bank account.

Even though not included in a person's net worth statement, human capital is VERY IMPORTANT because it provides a form of security. Formal education is one of the foundational cornerstones to increasing human capital. I am not inferring that acquiring education is a GUARANTEE that your human capital will be high. However, higher education can definitely give you an advantage in this arena. I know that there is some thinking out there that education isn't everything and that good experience and proper mentoring can be more valuable than formal education. Perhaps, in some cases, it can. Still, overall, it's a globally accepted principle that education is the key to increasing one's human capital.

Once someone has an education, it is important to protect and maintain their human capital with ongoing development. Courses, seminars, reading, and the like are examples of this.

Liabilities to Include:

Current Liabilities

These are liabilities based on a financial cycle or how often they are paid. For instance, are they paid weekly, bi-weekly or monthly? Most current liabilities are due and paid monthly, like a cellphone or utility bill.

Also considered a current liability is the current month's portion of any long-term liability. An example would be a monthly mortgage payment.

Long-Term Liabilities

These are liabilities that are due for payment for a more extended period than a monthly frequency - for instance, a 25-year mortgage or a 5-year car loan. Let's say that you own a home, and it has a $400,000 mortgage and a monthly mortgage payment of $1,000. The mortgage would be considered a long-term liability of $400,000. The monthly mortgage payment of $1,000 would be recorded as a current liability because it's due each month.

Current Liabilities (Due within 30 days)	Long Term Liabilities (Due beyond 30 days)
• Credit Card (s) • Utilities; Cellphone, Electricity, Cable, Natural gas, Oil, Water • Maintenance or Repair Services • Rent • Property Taxes • Insurance Premiums • Current Portion of Long Term loans (mortgage or consumer loans, etc.)	• Consumer Loans • Mortgage (s) • Investment loans • Student loans • Pledges • Amount owed on Leases

Asset and Liability Valuation

We've covered the different types of assets and liabilities. Let's now discuss how we value those assets and liabilities. There are four methods for doing the valuations.

1. **Market value**. This is the value someone else would pay for the asset in a fair arm's length transaction. "Arm's length" means a transaction between two parties who are independent of each other and do not have a close relationship. For instance, if I sell a property valued at $500,000 to my son for $100,000 to give him a good deal because of our relationship that is **NOT** an arm's length transaction.

2. **Historical cost**. This is the original price, or what you paid for the asset. For instance, I may have originally paid $250,000 for my home that is now worth $500,000.
3. **Depreciated cost.** Assets depreciate or lose value over time. This is the difference between what you originally paid, less a decreased value allowance. An example would be a car you originally paid $25,000 that has lost two years of depreciation ($10,000), therefore only worth $15,000, right now.
4. **Replacement cost.** This is the price paid to replace the asset in new condition. For example, if I had a television that I paid $1,000 for three years ago and lost it in a fire, the asset is obviously worth a lot less today. However, if I had to replace it, it may now cost $1,200 as the replacement cost.

Financial assets, such as real estate, pension plans and company stocks should be valued at market value. As you can see below from Brett's experience, it would not serve any purpose on the net worth statement to value the home at the original price. He would get somewhere close to the market price if he were to sell right now.

Brett, 47

I purchased a home back in 1990 for $225,000 and it seemed like a high price at the time. I thought I was crazy. Today, that same home is valued at $475,000 and is now fully paid. I'm sure glad I made that investment back then.

Camille, 37, and Brad, 31

We lost our home in the 2016 wildfire in Fort McMurray, Alberta. Let's just say the insurance claim was extensive and a difficult process to go through...I wouldn't wish it upon anyone. We had to itemize everything we lost. Pens, tools, clothes, cleaning products....You don't realize how much all those things you have in a home add up until you list them and look at the cost.

Personal use assets, such as linens, plates and kitchen utensils, are valuable, however, irrelevant for financial planning purposes. The only exception is for insurance reasons.

Certainly, identifying personal assets is a difficult process for anyone who suffers a loss, either through a natural disaster, vandalism, or theft. Of course, there are different ways to sell these articles online or at garage sales, but it is not likely that you can sell all of your personal use assets and convert them to cash. Therefore, they are not included in a net worth statement.

Other personal use assets like vehicles, larger maintenance equipment, etc., can be valued at market value, minus the costs associated with the sale.

Luxury assets should be valued at market value, which you would get for that asset if you sold it on the market. Additionally, people have different types of collections, like stamps, coins or sports cards. Depending on the type, there are ways to obtain the estimated value through an accredited appraisal. If this is not available, it's always better to use a more conservative amount rather than overstating the value.

Finally, **liabilities** should be valued at the *current obligation owing.*

So, what Does It Mean?

So now that we have our assets and liabilities valued correctly, we can calculate net worth.

ASSETS – Liabilities = Net Worth

As we are calculating net worth at a point in time (end of a month, quarter or year), the number means that if those assets were sold into cash and you paid off all the liabilities, this is the amount of money you would have left.

In a nutshell, we contribute to our financial assets for a period of time, from our jobs, self-employment, businesses or other income-generating methods. Then at some future point in time, we stop earning income and our ability to increase net worth diminishes.

The number itself simply tells you how much you and your family are worth financially. As discussed, you could compare yourself at another future point in time to see how you're progressing. There is, however, a couple of ratios that I like students and clients to review. These can provide additional insight into the net worth calculation.

1. Debt/equity ratio. This is the total debt (liabilities) divided by net worth (equity).

Total Debt
-------------------= D/E ratio
Equity (net worth)

In other words, it measures your total debt to equity or how many dollars (or other currency) of debt to every dollar (currency) of equity. For example, if your total debt was $240,000, and the equity was $100,000, it would be 2.4, or $2.40 of debt to every dollar of equity.

Simply looking at the number doesn't necessarily indicate whether it is good or not. This is where further analysis of the person's financial situation would be required, such as details of the life stage of the person, or the family, the type of debt and assets owned, and the like. For instance, a couple just starting out with a young family and a newly purchased home with a debt-equity ratio of 2.4 may be okay. However, if this was a couple getting ready for retirement, it may not be.

2. Current or Quick Ratio. This ratio is current assets divided by current liabilities.

Current Assets
-------------------- = Current or Quick ratio
Current Liabilities

This ratio simply measures your ability to pay or cover your current obligations. It is important because many people who incur large debt and cannot make their current payments tend to get further into debt due to the additional interest costs assessed when the balance is not paid. This could be a sign of or the start of more serious financial issues.

Current assets are cash or funds that are readily available to pay an obligation. Typically, these are cash balances in the bank. Although a person may have other financial assets, it's assumed that these assets like investments, emergency funds or retirement plans are not used to pay a current liability.

Current liabilities are those obligations that are due, typically within the next 30 days.

If the current assets are $4,000 and current liability $2,000, the current (quick) ratio would be 2.0. This means that the individual can easily cover the current month's obligation two times over.

Summary

In this chapter, we learned the importance of determining where a person stands financially at any given time. The Net Worth, or equity calculation, helps one understand their current financial position and can also be used to progress towards a future financial goal. It is simply calculated by **Assets - Liabilities = Net Worth**

We also reviewed the various types of assets and liabilities and how to value these in the Net Worth computation. Finally, we looked at a couple of ratios that could further help us understand some elements of Net Worth.

You're Worth a Lot More Than You Think
Action Step

Let's put this knowledge to practice now. Go to the *Fast Track to Prosperity Workbook* and using the framework in this chapter, calculate your Net Worth, Debt/Equity and Current (Quick) ratios as per the templates below. A downloadable Basic and Advanced version are available. Replace with your own currency if you use something other than dollars.

Were you surprised at your results? What conclusions can you make from your numbers and ratios? Are there any goals you want to develop using Net Worth, Debt/Equity (D/E) or Current ratios?

Here's where you can get these forms:
www.fasttrack2prosperity.com/bonus
Or scan this QR code with your phone camera.

Basic Version

PROSPERO
FINANCIAL SOLUTIONS LTD.

Personal Net Worth Financial Statement of:

as of:

Assets	**Amount in Dollars (Currency)**		**Current Assets**		
Cash - Bank accounts	$ -				
Investments	-				
Vehicle (s)	-				
Home Property	-				
Other assets (specify)	-				
Total Assets	**$ -**				
Liabilities	**Amount in Dollars**		**Current Liabilities**		
Current Debt (Credit cards, Accounts)	$ -		$ -	Total Current Liabilities	
Real Estate Mortgage (Principal Residence)	-				
Other liabilities (specify)	-				
Total Liabilities	**$ -**				
Net Worth	**$ -**				

Debt/Equity Ratio ________ **To 1**

Current/Quick Ratio ________

Signature: **Date:**

Advanced Version

PRO SPERO
FINANCIAL SOLUTIONS LTD.

Personal Net Worth Financial Statement of:

as of:

Assets	**Amount in Dollars (Currency)**		**Current Assets**	
Cash - Bank accounts	$ -			
Bonds	-			
Company Stocks - Public	-			
Mutual Funds	-			
ETF's (Exchange Traded Funds)	-			
Retirement Funds (RRSP's, Company Pension Plans, 401K's, etc.)	-			
TFSA's (Tax Free Savings Accounts- Canada)	-			
Vehicle (s)	-			
Real estate (Principal Residence)	-			
Real Estate (Rental Properties)	-			
Vacation Property	-			
Cryptocurrencies	-			
Jewelry, Collections, etc.	-			
Other assets (specify)	-			
Total Assets	**$ -**			
Liabilities	**Amount in Dollars**		**Current Liabilities**	
Current Debt (Credit cards, Accounts)	$ -		$ -	Total Current
Real Estate Mortgage (Principal Residence)	-			
Real Estate Mortgages (Rental Properties)	-			
Vehicle Loan	-			
Other liabilities (specify)	-			
Other liabilities (specify)	-			
Total Liabilities	**$ -**			
Net Worth	$ -			

Debt/Equity Ratio ______ **To 1**

Current/Quick Ratio ______

Signature: **Date:**

Financial Literacy Program, Level 2, November 2015

Financial Literacy Program, Level 1, July 2016

Financial Literacy Program, Level 2, November 2016

Financial Literacy Program, Level 2, June 2017

SECTION TWO – PLAN

THE ICE-CREAM KID DEVELOPS A PLAN

Update on Chilly Willy

I was escorted out of that area of the city by the "Dickie-Dee" police and went home contemplating the day's events. The thought of telling my superiors at "Chilly-Willy" or my parents what transpired didn't cross my mind. I had two choices, either quit for the summer and go back to delivering newspapers or take time to **PAUSE** and think how I would sell more ice cream. I chose the latter.

After several days of mulling this over, I decided that if I was going to be successful, I needed to revise my **"PLAN".** My goal was to earn a specific amount of money that summer, and I wasn't about to be side-tracked. Initially, I thought I would just go into another area of the city to avoid coming into contact with my nemesis. After a couple of shifts doing just that, I came across a sign close to a large school. The oversized banner was promoting a summer camp at that facility. I jotted down the phone number and contacted them that evening.

Apparently, this summer camp already had over 400 campers signed up, and kids from all over the city would attend the six-week event. My mind started working overtime as I saw the opportunity to potentially sell my ice cream to this enthusiastic crowd. I called the organizer the next day with my idea, and she was very open to my plan. She also told me that the camp wanted to buy a treat for all the kids that they would purchase from me once a week. In addition, I would also be allowed to set up my cart and sell it to the participants throughout the day.

So, the **"PLAN"** started to come together. I would have a consistent, targeted market during the weekdays at the summer camp and then go to other areas of the city on the weekends. I was so glad that I continued to pursue my goal rather than quit and go back to delivering newspapers.

I learned a critical lesson that summer. The importance of continuing to focus on my goals every day. I believe that because I did that, even in my own way as a young kid, I was more open to opportunities that I didn't even know existed. That day, the Universe was on my side when I came across that summer camp banner.

8

MONEY SHAME TO MONEY HOPE

As we move from the **PAUSE** to the **PLAN** portion of the process, this is the point where some people may experience difficulty transitioning. The **"PAUSE"** allows one to just take "a deep breath," take stock of things and think about the reason for their current financial status. Unfortunately, "Money shame" can creep in. This is where we begin to feel guilty for our past mistakes. Think of "what could have been" "what people will think," and this can start a downward spiral in our self-confidence.

I meet some interesting people in our industry at conferences and networking events. I was deeply moved by Dan and Brody's experience (not their real names). Dan was a successful Financial Planner, and Brody was his older brother who worked as a Machinist for a local company. Dan recalls that in 2012, he got a call from his brother a few weeks before Christmas. He sounded distressed, voice crackling and said he was in a tough spot. Brody went on to ask if he could borrow $50,000. This wasn't the first time his brother had needed a hasty advance, but this time he sensed something different in Brody's tone. Dan had never heard him so crushed and defeated. After a few questions and not wanting to feel "too nosy," Dan agreed to loan Brody money. The only condition was that, as the financial professional in the family, he wanted to meet with Brody and his wife to see what was really going on and provide some advice and help.

Dan went over to his brother and sister-in-law place a few days later to drop off the money and chat with them. He started off with the usual budget conversation with suggestions of selling off some toys, possibly downsizing and holding off on all those family vacations to Mexico and the Caribbean. Dan thought a little bit of a fiery scolding might get the two to "snap out" of their financial woes. Well, that didn't get anywhere as the couple started blaming each other for their past spending mistakes.

Dan often wondered when these two adults, with children in tow, would grow up and get their finances in order as it was affecting every aspect of their lives. After lending Brody the money, Dan didn't really hear from his brother for a few weeks. Just as well he thought, since that last encounter was certainly awkward and uncomfortable.

Christmas with the family was pretty tense that year, and Brody's distant and detached demeanor did not go unnoticed by the rest of the family. Several days later, Dan happened to call his father, and they chatted about the strained encounter during the holidays. His dad went on to say that Brody told him everything that was going on and was pretty upset with how Dan made him feel, especially in front of his wife. Brody felt hurt, embarrassed and wished he hadn't asked for the loan in the first place. Dan thought, of course he must have, and considered how he had money shamed his brother with his budget sermon and cost-cutting ideas. He thought he would just hang low and let things "cool off" a bit and allow Brody and his wife to sort out some of their financial issues.

A couple of months later, Dan received a devastating call from his sister. Brody had committed suicide earlier that day. He left behind two beautiful children, a 7-year old daughter, a 14-year-old son, and his wife of 16 years.

A few weeks after they buried Brody, Dan was asked to help his sister-in-law pick up the pieces of a shattered financial disaster. As he went through the den, he found a stack of overdue credit card bills and a foreclosure notice served to Brody several days before he took his life. Dan couldn't help but think about the day he went over to meet with Brody. He deeply regretted lecturing his brother on finances that day instead of being a caring, compassionate big brother who listened without judgement in order to help. It is something that haunts him every day of his life.

Money Shame

Dan realized his brother was trapped in a money shame vicious cycle. As we discussed in previous chapters, our core values run deep, and they shape the way we deal with finances. It's easy to internalize the money belief that our self-worth equals our net worth. One way to describe Money shame is:

That intense painful feeling of believing that we are imperfect and unworthy of love and community (belonging), based on our bank account balances, homes, cars or lifestyle.

It is no wonder that when we get into financial trouble, we are left believing that we're just lazy, stupid or just irresponsible with money.

This section of the "PLAN" is NOT about shaming anyone for past mistakes or feeling inferior for not properly planning and managing your finances.

We need to let go of past missteps and embrace what we can do going forward. If you are currently feeling money shame for any reason, please reach out to someone to simply talk. It doesn't have to be a financial person, just someone who will lend you an ear and not judge. You will find this liberating and start to heal from any money shame you may be feeling. Then, you can start looking at possible steps to start moving in the right direction; maybe set some 'quick-win' financial goals.

Summary

After you've "Paused" and determined where you are financially, you mustn't allow any money shame to thwart your progress forward. It is easy to be reminded of past financial decisions that didn't go as planned. This is especially true if it takes enormous steps and daily sacrifices to get yourself out of a "hole." Money shame thoughts and feelings can either come from external sources, like friends, family, co-workers, and media or just internally within ourselves.

I found it helpful to acknowledge these poor decisions and then make a strong declaration of your intent to move forward. In essence, it's a way of forgiving yourself for the past and reinforcing that you will not allow that to hinder your financial future.

Cindy and Mark's Acknowledgement and Declaration
We acknowledge that we made a poor financial decision in buying a $35,000 time-share in Mexico. This purchase often makes us feel remorseful and not confident in making other investment decisions. We declare that this decision will NOT defeat us, continue to cause anxiety in our lives us detract us from making better choices in the future.

____________	____________	____________
Cindy	Mark	Date

Here's a recent instance of financial remorse and their plan to avoid money shame.

Cindy, 42, and Mark, 47

About 10 years ago, we were on a vacation and attended a Time-share presentation. We knew it wasn't the best idea to buy a 2 week time-share in Mexico for $35,000 but we enjoyed the resort and figured we would come every year with the kids. And if we didn't come one year, we were encouraged by the rental policy the company had where we could just rent it out for that year. We also thought it would be a hedge against hotel prices in the future. We didn't have all the money so we got a loan for the balance. Well, currently, our annual maintenance fees have more than tripled from $200 to $650 since we bought it, the kids are older and don't want to go to same place every year, and we have never been able to rent it the years we didn't go. We tried selling it but there were no takers, so we're stuck with this asset that keeps losing money for us every year and every time we think about it, we feel awful and foolish for making such a decision. We've had our share of arguments about this over the years too!

Money Shame to Money Hope: Action Step

Now it's your turn. Go to the *Fast Track to Prosperity Workbook* and complete the "NO Money Shame Acknowledgement and Declaration" form. If you have any past regrets about financial choices you've made and want to lessen the chance of having money shame enter your thinking, take some time to acknowledge, declare and then be done with it. Don't allow any "garbage" thinking to crop back up in your mind. If it does, take out your worksheet and read it out loud and then move on.

This Declaration can be found at
www.fasttrack2prosperity.com/bonus
Or scan this QR code with your phone camera.

9

WHITE FLAG MOMENTS

For anyone who has experienced "money shame' and beat them self up over their poor financial decisions, it's crucial to 'pause' to understand the root cause of those decisions. Understanding what led to those decisions is critical to preventing a recurrence or possibly breaking a cycle of poor financial decisions and money shame.

As I've shared in the introduction, I have experienced “money shame”; I beat myself up over my poor financial decision at the time. It took me some time, and then I 'paused' in self-reflection to understand why I made those choices. This served a dual purpose in my own financial journey. First, it prevented me from "spiraling" back to a pattern of bad financial decisions and shame. Secondly, it prevented me from just shrugging off financially irresponsible behavior. Examples of my past thinking are:

"What's the use? I blew my budget this month anyway."

"An extra $2,000 on that renovation that's already costing me $20,000 won't kill me."

"I worked hard for my money. I deserve that"

"This looks like a good investment…I'm in…what's the worst-case scenario, I lose it all? I can make it up.

I know I'm not alone here. I talk to ordinary folks every day and students in our Financial Literacy Program (FLP) who have similar examples where we conveniently rationalize our overspending or under saving. So, what's going on is not a lack of financial knowledge, but an issue of slowly, day by day, transaction by transaction, giving up on our finances.

"White-Flag" Moments

For centuries, soldiers have been using white flags to signify surrender and defeat. For me, it's when I think there's no use in trying to make the right financial decision. So, I overspend, even though deep down I worry because I know it's not the best for my finances. I call this the "White-flag" moment.

Overspending and overextending ourselves can definitely happen with large purchases like a home or car. Still, as we previously discussed, we make more minor financial decisions every day. Make lunch or buy lunch? Meet friends for drinks this weekend or not? Renew that magazine or streaming service or not? How much do we spend on our friends' wedding gift: $50, $100, $200? On top of that, add the usual weekly groceries, insurance payments, kid's school supplies, new clothes, grooming and so on. Many of these can be White-flag Moments for us. Most of these choices seem small and inconsequential. But like the saying, "death by a thousand cuts," our finances can be ruined little by little, over time.

I've had my share of "White-flag" moments in my time. Some small and some, like in my introduction, are very consequential. These were instances where I went ahead and spent money on something I knew I couldn't afford or couldn't afford to lose, yet I carried on with the decision. What made me succumb to the pressure to spend? I consider myself a rational and logical person (well, most of the time). I needed to understand the underpinning of this thinking.

Without avoiding these "White-flag" moments, I would be at risk of continuing to make poor and devastating financial decisions that would affect my financial future. Like trying to cover a stab wound with a Band-Aid, it's not going to work. To effectively treat the injury (or deal with the problem), you need 'pause' to understand the source of the problem and then work on a plan for an effective solution.

It is interesting to note that debt levels continue to rise across North America, even with all the readily available financial information on the internet, social media or apps. Knowing the mechanics of picking stocks, purchasing real estate or trading foreign or cryptocurrencies is futile if there isn't money at the end of the month to invest. This "Plan" section is about having and implementing a plan that will enable you to have the funds to prosper in the short and long term.

Recognizing Your Triggers

So, what are the triggers that cause us to have "White-flag" moments? For many people, it's that desire or urge to "keep up with Joneses," a term often used to infer overspending or over-extending to keep pace with our neighbors' lifestyle.

It's normal to compare ourselves with those individuals who are like us to see how we measure up financially. In other facets of life like sports, career, or personal accomplishments, looking up to those who have what we want can be a source of encouragement, focus and determination to achieve your own goals. So, looking over at Joneses and saying, "Hey, we should do what they do to get our finances under control," or "How were they able to pay off their mortgage so quickly?" This is healthy and strongly encouraged. We can learn well from those who are successful.

However, it becomes problematic when 'keeping up' means buying a large home or a new car that is more expensive than can reasonably be afforded. Or going on expensive vacations on credit because our friends travel. This is where financial problems can "snowball."

Everyone has a different concept of what it means to live a successful and fruitful life. As discussed at length in the Goals section, our core values ultimately formulate our goals. Suppose we can identify those triggers that cause the "white-flag" moments. In that case, we can better predict when they may occur and, more importantly, avoid or mitigate them.

Jackie and Brian came to see me for some financial coaching. They recently celebrated the arrival of their second child, and Jackie was on parental leave. They were relying on Brian for the primary source of income and were drowning in debt. They explained, "A couple of years ago, we decided to buy a home, after renting for several years. Many of our friends, with young families, seemed to be on the home-ownership track, and we thought it was time to get on that train, as well. It seemed that whenever we got together with our friends, everyone was talking about their home building plans, issues with contractors and picking out colors for the kitchen cabinets. We felt a bit left out, and we just started thinking more and more about taking the big step to purchasing our own home."

Jackie and Brian have good incomes and could comfortably afford a $350,000 home based on their finances. "We wanted some upgrades to the basic home specs and thought about having more kids, so we eventually ended up buying a 4 bedroom, rather than 3 bedroom home…It cost $475,000." Finances would be tight, but they figured they could manage, with Brian advancing professionally in his company.

Looking back, this was their "white-flag" moment. As time went on, there always seemed to be some unexpected costs. One child was expensive, but two were additionally constraining. Even when Brian got a promotion, it wasn't nearly enough to offset all the additional costs they incurred. Unfortunately, they were now in a position where they had to make some significant sacrifices to financially get back on track. As harsh as it was, one option was selling the home and moving into another lower-cost neighborhood. The consequences of white flag moments can get us into financial issues down the road.

Social Media Trigger

As if it wasn't difficult enough trying to keep our expectations in check, social media comes along and it kicks it up a notch. Social media not only influences overspending, but it can also intensify "Keeping Up with the Jones" and the F.O.M.O. (Fear of Missing Out). I'm not advocating a social media ban, and there's nothing wrong with celebrating accomplishments, travels and the like.

Still, we need to keep this intense information and image overload in check. We are bombarded by personally targeted ads urging us to spend while we're scrolling through our friend's achievements, restaurant visits and vacation experiences.

It's no wonder that a study by Allianz Life found a 61% of

millennials said that they've had feelings of inadequacy about their lives because of what they saw on social media, and 57% said that social media causes them to spend money due to the fear of missing out.[1] Additionally, Credit Karma found that 39% of millennials have gone into debt just to keep up with their friends.[2] By the way, this is not confined to the above age demographic. Generation X'ers down to Baby Boomers are also falling into the trap of the 'fear of missing out' on spending because of over exposure to media.

Scroll through your social media feeds, and you'll see some remarkable achievements by your friends and notable influencers. The perfect picture is with them in an exotic location, driving in a new car with the wind blowing through… well, it was a lovely hairstyle. Then, watching a few five-star chefs carve pieces of meat into slick filets in a fancy restaurant. Those photos only reveal part of what happened. As a popular radio programming announcer used to say, "And now for the rest of the story." A bill comes along with these events, often outlasting the initial experience. You notice that no one ever posts their credit card statement or their mortgage balance for everyone to see to put things into perspective.

In addition to the social pressures that can come from the F.O.M.O. and the Joneses, there is also the element of targeted ads. It's no secret that social media companies collect information on our searches and visited sites and then send us specific ads to appeal to our age, gender, interests and income level. For instance, if you've been browsing Instagram posts on cars, you are likely to get ads from car and finance companies to automobile cleaning products. And the ads are unrelenting.

I recently provided my email for a free download report on an exercise program offered by a popular trainer on Instagram. Shortly after, every platform I was on: Facebook, Instagram, Tumblr… within the next two or three posts on each social media platform came the ad for the exercise program. This is not to mention the barrage of emails, which

I still haven't unsubscribed to. We don't stand a chance with that type of exposure and technology advancements. It's like trying to navigate through an area planted with land mines. Unless we recognize the danger and carefully steer through it, we will succumb to its perils.

Here is an excellent example of social media or online shopping triggers. Tamara came to see me one day for some financial coaching. Her credit card debt was over $5,000, and she could only afford to make the monthly minimum payment due to her other financial commitments. I asked her to explain to me how she got into the situation. Not to money-shame her, but so that she could acknowledge the problem, and then we would put a plan in place. "I guess I love shopping online," she said. "I don't have to go into a mall and try the clothes on, and there's usually some pretty good sales on with coupons and special offers."

She also told me that her credit card information was saved on various sites, so she didn't have to reenter her information all the time. I asked if she was serious about getting her finances in order, and she said, "Yes, of course." When I told her that we would have to take some pretty drastic measures, she looked at me like a puppy who had been gnawing on a bone, and I was about to take it out away. This was the plan:

- Limit her social media to a maximum of one hour per day,
- Delete her credit card information from all apps and online retailers,
- Cancel her monthly subscription to services and products she hasn't used in the last three months, and
- Unsubscribe to all retailers sending her emails.

She agreed to the plan and went off to implement the

items. After six months, we met again to review progress. "It was hard at first," she reported, "but I found it easier after a couple of weeks." The debt had been reduced by half, and she hadn't purchased any additional products other than food and some personal necessities. "I didn't realize how I just bought stuff because I felt down at times, and the way I set it up made it so easy to do. I'm glad I 'paused' and put these measures in place."

Common Triggers: "The Rock" Element

I've seen numerous articles and blogs about celebrity culture and the pressure to unachievable and unrealistic lives of perfect bodies, exciting travels, fine dining and leisure time toys. There is some element of wanting to emulate a famous celebrity by their clothes or exercise regime. Still, we know that most of us can't realistically achieve their lifestyles.

Suppose Dwayne "The Rock" Johnson bought a Cessna Citation jet to globetrot around the world or a $20 million home in California. Would you feel inadequate and unfulfilled in life for not owning the same? Probably not. As a successful movie star, he's in a different category than most of us. We're usually not comparing ourselves to such an extravagant lifestyle. However, it is natural to compare ourselves to people in our work or social circle. These are the individuals we have contact every day in our jobs or neighborhoods, or online.

The mistaken thinking is that since these folks have similar jobs, income levels, or kids, they are doing well financially. But we don't know the details of their finances. They could be living paycheck to paycheck or very deep in debt like Jackie and Brian. I've done my share of income tax returns over the years. You definitely get a clearer picture of where people are actually at financially, compared to what it may seem from the outside, looking in.

Alternatively, a wealthy family member could have been

partially paid off that beautiful home, or a company housing program benefit may have subsidized the purchase. The main point here is that since you don't know what the financial health is for anyone in your work or social circle, comparing yourself to them is futile. It's no different than trying to compare yourself to "The Rock"… It DOES NOT MATTER. This simple but profound truth could save you years of heartaches, struggles and emotional pain.

Summary

Individuals with money problems probably got there over time. The effect of poor financial choices, which individually didn't seem material at the time, can add up quickly if not monitored or controlled. The "White-flag" moments are those instances we give up on our finances, thinking that "this small decision won't matter." But they do, and understanding those triggers are imperative to avoid financial difficulties. Many want to keep up with the Joneses or have the F.O.M.O., so they spend money they don't have or make poor investment choices.

Social media and comparisons between our lives and those we see in our online feeds can fuel inadequacy and trigger "White-flag" moments. Limiting time on the internet or social media networks and realizing that we don't know the finer details of people's finances can help us mitigate those feelings of not having enough.

White Flag Moments: Action Step

Let me hand it over to you now. Go to the *Fast Track to Prosperity Workbook* and complete the exercise on "White-flag" moments. In this exercise, you will recall any "White-flag" moments that you've made in the past, acknowledge and then move on. Then, you will identify those triggers that may lead you to make "White-flag" decisions, so you can prevent making them in the future.

Finally, you will think about the amount of time you are spending on social media each week and consider taking some steps to curb it, if required.

These exercises can be found at www.fasttrack2prosperity.com/bonus
Or scan this QR code with your phone camera.

10

THE DREADED "B" WORD....AND THE SOLUTION TO BUDGETING

In previous chapters, we've established that there is no shame in past poor financial decisions, only lessons to leverage those learnings so we don't repeat them. Recognizing triggers that may cause us to overspend brings us to the part of actually planning our finances. Yes, we have **"Paused"**, and now we are ready to **"Plan"**. Planning is controlling your cash flow; that is, money coming in and going out.

Everything we've covered so far about core values, goals and determining net worth won't mean much if you don't have control over your cash flow. When we know where our money is going, we feel more confident in the way we are managing our cash and, ultimately, our financial future.

For this reason, this element is probably the most crucial part of personal finances. After all, you can't invest money and have it work for you for future use if there isn't anything at the end of the month to invest. Having control over your finances doesn't mean knowing where every penny, centavo or peso is being spent. Similar to when we were determining net worth, this isn't an accounting exercise that will be audited; however, you need to understand your cash flow well.

The Dreaded "B" Word

What do you think is the most dreaded word in personal finance circles? From my experience, it's **"Budgeting"**. When I coach people in tough shape financially, it usually calls for drastic measures. The mention of the word 'budget' can cause people to squirm, profusely sweat or concede that they've tried it before, and it DOESN'T work. And it's no wonder. We've been conditioned to think that budgeting is the only way to really control our money.

We've heard the mantra...Track your historical spending for a few months into different categories, estimate your monthly expense and then track your expenses against those estimates. The truth is, most people that follow this process are doomed to fail. Why?

Take weight-loss diets as an example. Many times, people trying to lose weight go on crazy, restrictive, fad diets and end up not achieving their goal. They may lose some weight initially, but most times, they gain the weight back and even put on more weight than they originally started from. This is often a vicious cycle of diet, weight loss, weight gain, and then repeat the cycle again. Each time the weight returns, they feel like a failure which reinforces their inability to deal with the issue (in this case, losing weight). Why? The plan is unrealistic and unsustainable, so people just give up and think they can never achieve their goal and wave their 'white flag.'

Budgeting is no different. I've seen it many times, over and over again, and financial advisors continue to "beat the budget drum." I'm not saying that it fails all the time, but for most people I know who have tried traditional budgeting, they usually give up after a few months, or the next time an unforeseen expense crops up and "blows away" all their plans.

Additionally, in this age of technological sophistication, there's an overabundance of apps and spreadsheet templates to help you "budget." Unfortunately, most work by negative reinforcement. Imagine some developer has programmed an app to alarm you when you're not on track to hit your toiletries goal for the month. In other words, it tells you that you're on track to overspend on your toiletries target. Not only is this restrictive, but it constantly reminds you of financial choices you can't make. And we all know what happens when someone tells us we can't do something; we want to do it even more. Whether it is restrictive diets or budgets, rigid rules rarely work, as seen by one of our students in the Program.

Lionel was all excited about a new budgeting tool he came across. He had previously tried other methods like collecting receipts and then tracking the expenses, but those methods always seemed to fall short. So, when he was introduced to this new app while scrolling through his social media feed, he felt convinced that it would definitely work. After all, the eight-minute ad said so, and it came with a 60-day money back guarantee.

At the end of each month, after Lionel input every expense, the app would produce a litany of colorful charts and spreadsheets. There was so much information presented that he had difficulty determining what was actually helpful. After a few months, it became just another distasteful chore, and Lionel cancelled his monthly subscription.

Lionel explained, "It got to the point where I would be out with my wife for dinner, and we would argue about how much the night was costing us because of the "cautionary" report I received in my inbox earlier that afternoon." Another example he relayed went like this, "Once we went to buy the kids their school supplies, I caught myself penny-pinching on a backpack so I could meet the monthly goal." Lionel felt exasperated at what the app was restricting him from doing, especially when it created a situation where hitting the target was more important than spending a few extra dollars to support his girl's back over a long school year. Lionel said to me, "I just scraped it at that point."

Traditional budgeting is too restrictive and often leads to "white-flag" moments like the example above. A restrictive system like traditional budgeting isn't reflective of our daily lives. The demands of everyday life are rarely constant and straightforward. Like a bamboo that bends but doesn't break, any successful spending and savings plan must be flexible and malleable to what life throws us. After all, life is short, and we're allowed to enjoy the fruits of our labor in a financially responsible but not restrictive manner. It's not anyone's business how you choose to spend your money or save it, for that matter. **The only condition is that you're spending money you can afford to spend.**

So, if we want to say "adios" to budgeting, we have to come up with an alternate solution. A plan that allows us control of our cash flow while looking out for our financial security, now and in the future. In the following chapters, we will determine the amount of money we can spend that doesn't jeopardize our long-term financial well-being. Once you've mastered this simple but effective planning tool, you can forget about budgeting forever.

What's the Answer to Budgeting?

If budgeting doesn't work for most people, but we still need to be in control of our finances, what's the answer? At the end of the day, being financially responsible means meeting your commitments. These include current ones like paying your bills and saving enough for the future.

If you are doing this, does it really matter that you've spent more on shampoo and hair grooming versus lunches in a particular month? Absolutely not. You're living within your means, controlling your cash flow, and meeting commitments, so go ahead and spend as you please.

Growing up, I was a Boy Scout, and I remember hiking in the beautiful Kananaskis area nestled in the magnificent Canadian Rocky Mountains. After hiking for several kilometers, we came to the end of a trail. There a sign read:

A pretty clear picture of the consequences of not following the caution sign. What if we had a financial caution sign to warn us when we could or could not spend money? Of course, it wouldn't have to be as dramatic as, "crossing the line entails falling into the financial abyss."

That sign is something I call the **"Spending Margin"**. This is the amount of money that you can spend on anything you want because you've already met your high-priority commitments for the month. The Spending Margin separates the money you can spend from the money you cannot. It's like saying, "go ahead, you can afford this."

The Spending Margin

In developing a spending plan that works, there are six categories to look at:

- Net Take-Home Pay
- Fixed Expenses
- Important Savings
- Interim Savings
- Retirement Savings
- Spending Margin

Your income will be allocated to one of these groups to determine the money assigned to your spending margin.

1. **Net take-home pay** is the amount of money that is deposited into your account by your employer.
2. **Fixed expenses** are those costs that usually don't change from month to month or period to period. As such, these can be more easily estimated. Fixed expenses typically make up the most significant percentage of our total spend, including mortgage or rent payments, car payments and utility bills. Since they are constant every period, a periodic review to see if they can be lowered is an excellent strategy to reduce your fixed cost structure.
3. **Important savings** is money set aside to help us improve our overall financial well-being. Important

savings are typically used to pay down debt, save for a down-payment on a home or rental property, **eliminate** a student loan, etc. These are an essential part of any plan to progress your financial position. Individuals who get into excessive debt have a higher portion of their income that must go to reduce this obligation. In turn, this leaves them with less money for the other categories below.

4. **Interim savings** is intended for a short period of time. It's for items that keep us out of debt when we make larger purchases, and for emergencies, vacations, etc. For instance, if we set up an emergency fund that we **contribute** to monthly, the money is available when the furnace or air conditioning fails. It can also be used to plan for more minor expenses like children's birthday parties or weddings that you have to buy gifts for.
5. **Retirement savings** is a separate category, as our long-term finances are an essential part of what we will consume in the future. Again, depending on your core values, some people may place more of their current income for retirement purposes than others.
6. The **Spending Margin** is what's left outstanding. If you think about it, now that you've taken care of the fixed expenses, important, interim and retirement commitments, whatever is left over, is what should be guilt-free spending.

The Spending Margin is important in that there is now no need to further budget. This should be "music to the ears" of all of us that dislike budgeting. If someone wants to spend this extra cash on expensive dinners this month, no big deal. After all, the mortgage, utility bills, children's education and retirement have been taken care of. Do you see how this can remove all the guilt, inadequacies and "white flag" moments that are often associated with hard-core, restrictive budgeting?

Calculating Your Spending Margin

Step 1: What's Your After-Tax Income?

The first step in the process is to calculate the income that is deposited into your bank account every month. As we said before, we're not doing accounting here, so there is no need to get into the "nitty-gritty" of all the detailed deductions that come off your gross pay. We're interested in the money we have to operate in the period.

For most **employees**, it's the amount on your pay or deposited into your account. Simply multiply your net pay by two to get the monthly amount if you're paid twice a month. For instance, if Chen's net pay is $2,500, then his monthly after-tax income is $5,000 ($2,500 x 2). There may be instances where there are more deductions at a point of the year than others. Don't worry; it won't make a difference if the deductions are minimal. If you think they are material, simply add up your 24 pays for the year and divide by 12 to get a more accurate number.

Similarly, if you are paid biweekly and get 26 pays a year, add up the total pay for the year and divide by 12 to get a net monthly amount.

Pay	Net Pay	Total Net Annual Pay	# of Pays/Month	Monthly After Tax Income
Twice/month	$ 2,500	$ 60,000	2	$ 5,000
Monthly	$ 5,000	$ 60,000	1	$ 5,000
Bi-weekly	$ 2,308	$ 60,000	2	$ 4,615
Weekly	$ 1,154	$ 60,000	4	$ 4,615

For **self-employed** individuals, it's still possible to calculate net pay, but it's a little different than that of an employee. The simplest way to do this is to take last year's net pay results and make any adjustments for the upcoming year. Alternatively, you could also forecast the amounts for the following year. Either way, you may have to make changes to this number as you receive your net pay.

Step 2: What Are Your Fixed Expenses?

Fixed expenses reoccur every period, whether monthly, quarterly or annually. The regularity of these expenses makes them very predictable and, therefore, easier to plan or budget for.

Examples of some fixed expenses include:

- Mortgage or payments
- Insurance (home, auto, tenant's insurance, life, critical illness)
- Property tax
- Car loan or lease payment
- Utilities
- Gym membership
- Mobile cellphone
- Subscriptions (magazines, apps, streaming services, etc.)
- Charitable donations
- Daycare
- Spousal and child support
- Transportation costs (bus, etc.)
- Consumer loan payments
- Parking (if a standard monthly rate)

If you're having trouble determining if an expense is fixed or not, just think of those costs that are predictable and certain to occur over the period. A fast-food kiosk in a mall will have a fixed rent regardless of the number of lunch sales they generate that month. For us personally, fixed expenses are commitments that are roughly the same amount every period and non-negotiable.

If a cost fluctuates from month to month, it is not a fixed expense for our purposes in this section. That's why we've included daycare but not food or transportation. This is not whether you will incur the specific expense but more about whether <u>you can predict it with some accuracy</u>. We have food costs every month, but one month we may spend $700 and the next $900 because we stocked up on meat or other more expensive food items.

Your bank and/or credit statements will quickly reveal those expenses that are fixed and those that tend to fluctuate. An example of these would be items like groceries, gas or toiletries. Rarely are these predictable with any amount of accuracy because they vary from month to month.

For expenses incurred quarterly or annually, add up the total yearly cost and divide by 12. Similarly, utility bills may be higher in the winter months, so just add the previous year's charges and divide by 12. In this manner, you will have some months where you're saving more than what you are billed for, but this balance will slowly build up and come in handy for those higher-cost months. That is, unless you are on a regulated monthly plan, in which case it will be a fixed monthly cost.

Here's an example of Chen and Jing Wang's fixed expense profile.

Chen and Jing Wang's Bank and Credit Card Statement		
Monthly Transactions	**Amount**	**Predictable Yes/No**
Mortgage	$ 750	Yes
Car Insurance	$ 90	Yes
Streaming Service	$ 25	Yes
Life Insurance	$ 75	Yes
Cellphone	$ 50	Yes
Parking	$ 40	Yes
Groceries	$ 275	No
Gym Membership	$ 30	Yes
Gas	$ 75	No
Furniture Loan payment	$ 50	Yes
Student Loan payment	$ 100	Yes
Clothing	$ 135	No
Other Predictable Transactions		
Home Insurance	$840 annually	Yes
Water, Electricity	$960 annual total cost	Yes
Property Tax	$1,500 annual cost	Yes

Chen and Jing Wang's Fixed Expenses		
Mortgage	$ 750	
Car Insurance	$ 90	
Streaming Service	$ 25	
Life Insurance	$ 75	
Cellphone	$ 50	
Parking	$ 40	
Gym Membership	$ 30	
Furniture Loan payment	$ 50	
Student Loan payment	$ 100	
Home Insurance	$ 70	$840 / 12 months
Water, Electricity	$ 80	$960 / 12 months
Property Tax	$ 125	$1,500 / 12 months
Total	**$ 1,485**	

So, after this simple analysis, you can see the Wang's fixed expenses are $1,485. As we discussed earlier, this is the cost structure for this couple's finances that are committed and set to be paid every month. There is nothing to say they shouldn't be looking to try and reduce these fixed costs by taking actions like renegotiating premiums on the car and home insurance or eliminating the streaming service altogether. Any decrease in fixed costs can substantially impact the bottom line because the monthly savings are multiplied many times over the year. For instance, a $40 per month reduction in car insurance is $480 per year ($40 x 12).

From my experience, fixed expenses can be as high as 50-55% of net take-home pay. When you get over this amount, it means that more than half of your income is already spoken for and doesn't leave much for the rest of the monthly expenses we still need to consider. In this case, if we use the $5,000 take-home pay example, this is at 30% ($1,485 ÷ $5,000), so he's well below that acceptable range.

Step 3: What Are Your Important Savings?

Important savings are those that have the most significant impact on your net worth. They either decrease the liabilities (debt) you owe or increase your own assets. For debt reduction, this is the payment over and above any fixed expense obligation of the loan. In our example, the Wangs may decide that they want to increase the amount of the furniture loan repayment, so they put aside an additional $25 for this debt over and above the $50 they already make as a fixed expense.

Here are some examples of Important Savings:

- Paying down a mortgage (either lump sum or doubling up on the fixed expense portion)
- Paying down a loan (Line of Credit (L.O.C.), furniture, Student loan, etc.)

- Paying down a car loan
- Saving for a down payment on real estate (whether for personal home or rental property)
- Saving for children's education fund
- Savings for a vacation or a particular project

Another feature of this category is that you may be making this payment only for the short to medium term. For example, a couple decides they want to pay off their entire student loan in three years. Once they reach their goal, that period of savings will come to an end.

With Important savings, you consciously set aside funds to increase your short and long-term financial wellbeing. With this in mind, you should feel good about this part of the "**Plan**" because you are being financially responsible and directly controlling your cash flow. There is something powerful about knowing you have taken care of important financial decisions while still enjoying and living in the present.

Calculating Important Savings for Debt Repayments

If you have a goal of paying off any debt, you need to know how much you're going to put towards it every period. You don't simply want to use the minimum payment required by the lender, as this is where they make their money. For example, if you only pay the minimum amount on your credit card statement, you will pay 18-28 % on the remaining balance until it is all paid off. More about that in the '**Prosper**' section.

Dividing the total amount of the loan by the number of months won't suffice because one needs to consider the effect on the interest of the outstanding portion of the loan. Once you have a goal in mind, use the ***Loan Calculator – Debt Repayment*** like the one described in the Resources section at the end of this book to determine the additional payment amount you could make.

For instance, if the Wang family has a furniture loan of $4,000 with a 15% annual interest rate and a $50 minimum payment and they want to pay it off in 5 years (60 months), that information is plugged into the ***Loan Calculator – Debt Repayment***, and it generates a payment of $95.16. To calculate the Interim savings component, subtract the minimum payment or the fixed expense ($50) from the $95.16, and the Wangs will have to set aside an additional $45.16 a month to pay the loan off in 5 years.

Financing Larger Important Projects

Some other important plans may include saving for your children's education or accumulating enough funds to purchase a home or rental property. Some folks don't want to incur any debt to go on a vacation, buy new furniture or do a renovation, so this is an excellent way to save and have the money before making the actual purchase.

The time frame you've set for your goal will determine how to calculate the amount required on every month. If it's a shorter-term goal (1-3 years), simply dividing the amount required by the number of months will suffice. For instance, if you want to plan for a $6,000 kitchen renovation in the next 2 years, you will have to save $250 a month. ($6,000 ÷ 36 months = $250). Placing the funds in a simple savings account earning the current interest rate will serve its purpose.

If the goal is a longer-term project (greater than 3 years), like savings for a child's education or a down payment for a home, you will want to invest the funds as they accumulate over this long-time span. Chen and Jing Wang wish to buy a rental property down the road and will have to save $40,000 over the next 10 years. Using the simple calculation, they would need to save $333 per month ($40,000 ÷ 120 months =

$333.33). However, since it is a more extended period of time that they're saving for, they should invest the funds and make some gains on the amount. This would mean that they don't have to contribute as much every period.

A ***Savings Goal Calculator*** like the one described in the Resources section at the end of this book will help you determine the actual amount you will need to save, taking the rate of return into account. A conservative return in a balanced mix of assets (see Chapter 15) should generate about 5% per year in our example. Using these numbers, the amount required to save for this down payment is now $265.03; therefore, $68.30 less than the simple calculation ($333.33- $265.03). That's over $800 less per year that could be used for other savings or expenses in the family.

Chen and Jing Wang's Important Savings		
Furniture Loan (above minimum)	$	45
Kitchen Renovation	$	250
Down Payment for Home	$	265
Total	**$**	**560**

Step 4: What Are Your Interim Savings?

This next category is also savings, but it's different from the previous group we just reviewed. Although Interim savings do not necessarily increase your net worth, they are an integral part of your financial wellness. This type of savings can help us avoid getting into permanent debt as we experience unplanned or spikes in expenses.

I have seen many people give up on their budgeting or spending plan because of an unexpected or planned expense that costs more than anticipated. The furnace needs replacing, the car has more maintenance issues than planned and increases for kid's birthday parties to attend to now that you're in a new neighborhood. All of these things happen in life but can cause a lot of stress on the financial side if we're not prepared.

The following are examples of Interim savings:

- Birthday parties, weddings and special holiday spending
- Vacations
- Children's activities like music or sports
- Car and home repair/maintenance
- Health costs (if no insurance or insurance does not cover)
- Emergency fund

For the anticipated expenses, simply divide the goal by the number of months the funds are required. The Wangs have a special family vacation planned in two years that will cost $4,000; therefore, they will have to stash away $167 ($4,000 ÷ 24 months) per month to reach their goal. Similarly, add up last year's costs for the kids' seasonal sports or music activities and divide by 12 months to determine how much you will require. Let's say it's been $400 per year per child. The Wangs have two children, so it comes out to $66.67 per month ($800 ÷ 12 months). Gifts for events were $600 last year. This would equate to $50 ($600 ÷ 12 months).

The Emergency Fund

Not all interim costs are predictable like those we reviewed in the previous section. Eventually, everyone experiences some type of unplanned expense or an emergency. Having an emergency fund gives you the peace of mind to know that should you encounter an issue; you can worry about how to deal with the emergency itself rather than worrying about how you're going to afford to pay for it. Some examples are losing a job or needing a major repair on your house.

When it comes to items like car and home repairs, a quick review of the last two-year average cost divided by 12 months will give you a reasonable estimate. Obviously, if you recently purchased a new car or did a major repair on the home, like a roof or windows, adjust your projections accordingly. House and car maintenance has averaged $3,000 per year for the last couple of years for Chen and Jing. Therefore, the estimated savings to cover this would be $250 ($3,000 ÷ 12 months).

Planning for a job loss entails a little more work. While a person's emergency fund will vary from person to person, most financial experts agree that an adequate emergency reserve should hold between three to eight months of monthly expenses. These should cover the fixed costs plus some additional amount for basic living. Depending on your personal situation, if there is a second income in the household, other income from investments or other sources (i.e. Rental properties, government or child/ spousal support, etc.), that will determine how many months of expenses are sufficient.

In our example, the fixed expenses were $1,485 plus, let's assume another $1,515 for other living expenses (groceries, grooming, gas, etc.). This would equate to $3,000 a month. Again, depending on each case, the emergency fund could range between $9,000 (3 x 3 months) to $24,000 (3 x 8 months).

The good news is that this doesn't have to be done overnight. One can start small and slowly work up to the ultimate goal. Another good option is to set this up as a smaller goal, like $1,000 to $2,000. This smaller goal is much easier to reach and allows you to feel accomplished once you reach this important milestone in your finances. Again, for the Wangs, it comes out to $250 per month ($3,000 ÷ 12 months).

Total Interim Savings

The Wangs have a total of $784 of Interim savings in their plan. By setting aside this amount every month, they will not only save for spikes in spending and unforeseen emergencies, but it will give them a sense of peace that these costs are accounted for.

Chen and Jing Wang's Interim Savings		
Vacation Fund	$	167
Kid's Activities	$	67
Event Gifts	$	50
Home/Car Repairs	$	250
Emergency Fund	$	250
Total	**$**	**784**

Step 5: What Are Your Retirement Savings?

This portion of the plan is probably the most difficult to estimate. Surging medical advancements increase life expectancy worldwide, and people live longer into their retirement years. Therefore, savings for this stage of life is becoming increasingly more important. Many folks I talk to can estimate their short-term savings needs but have difficulty coming up with the appropriate number for retirement. After all, if you listen to some financial advisors, it's easy to think you require more than you actually do, so that causes individuals to work longer and save more than they really need. On the other hand, it's just as common to not save enough because we're living longer. So, what's a person to do?

Well, we can still arrive at a reasonable forecast, but it will take a little more brainpower. In addition, this should be part of your Core Value assessment and goal setting that we reviewed in previous chapters. Here are some of the **Retirement factors** that will determine the estimate:

- When do you plan to retire? The earlier the date, the more you will need in the pot.
- What other assets do you have that can be converted to cash and used in retirement (i.e. rental properties, stocks, etc.)?
- The performance and expected return of those assets. Poor performance and a volatile stock could significantly affect how much you have at retirement.
- How much do you want to leave to your family, charitable organizations, etc.?
- When do/did you start putting money away for retirement? The later in life, the more that is currently required.
- A personal family situation can include a wide variety of circumstances such as marital status, financial support for other family members, whether there is a second income contributing to the retirement fund, to name a few.
- Is your employer providing some sort of Pension that would ultimately reduce the amount you personally have to save for retirement?
- Are there any Government pensions or support you will be entitled to in retirement?
- Although difficult to estimate, are there any potential inheritances to consider?
- Will you own your own home or have a mortgage in retirement?

A rule-of-thumb used by many financial experts is to save at least 10 percent of your gross income for retirement. Gross income is your annual salary before any deductions instead of the net take-home pay we calculated in Step 1. For example, if Jing Wang was 30 years old and made $60,000 gross income annually, she would need to save $6,000 a year or $500 per month ($6,000 ÷ 12 months). Now, as Jing's income increases, so does her contribution. If her gross annual income increases to $66,000, she would put aside $6,600 (or $550 per month.)

If we assume Jing contributes $5,000 per year for 35 years and achieves a 5% return, her retirement fund will grow to $556,489. (As per the ***Investment Inflation Calculator*** found in the Resources section at the end of the book). This is a great strategy, but Jing would have to temper this plan with the retirement factors discussed above and make changes accordingly.

Again, Jing started contributing at age 30 to accumulate this amount. If someone starts contributing later in life, the 10% could easily increase to 20% or more of gross income.

As you look at these numbers and think about how you could possibly have enough to contribute 10-20% of gross income in addition to living day to day, don't despair! Put a plan in place, and we will look at other ways to reduce expenses and increase returns on investments later.

Jing Wang's Retirement Savings	
Retirement Savings	$ 500
Total	**$ 500**

Step 6: What Is Your Spending Margin?

Hey, we're finally at the last step! Now that we've calculated the net take-home pay and subtract fixed expenses, and important, interim and retirement savings, the remaining balance is the **Spending Margin**.

	Spending Margin	
Take-Home Pay		**$ 5,000**
Fixed Expenses	$ 1,485	
Important Savings	$ 560	
Interim Savings	$ 784	
Retirement Savings	$ 500	
Subtotal		**$ 3,329**
Spending Margin		**$ 1,671**

For the Wangs, the $3,329, made up of the fixed expenses, Important, Interim and Retirement Savings are spoken for and should not be spent. The $1,671 Spending Margin is the amount that is available for spending on what they choose for that month.

This is the only **CAUTION SIGN** you will ever need. Once the bills are paid, and your savings are taken care of, who cares how you spend your Margin? Didn't we say it is your money and that every person and family is different? Just know that you should not go over $1,671. Continuing to exceed this amount could be cause for a financial EMERGENCY 9-1-1.

When I was going through school, I would feel guilty about going out with friends or taking a break because I thought I should be studying instead. Well, if you plan your finances this way, you shouldn't feel any pressure or guilt about spending within your margin.

Isn't this better than budgeting or an app that tracks every dollar or an alarm slapping you on the wrist because you bought an iced Frappuccino with extra cream? Again, the numbers will vary from month to month, especially at the beginning when you're setting up the plan, but over time should settle, and you will begin to clearly see the benefits.

It is also a good idea to review the **Plan** a couple times a year to see if you can reduce some fixed costs or adjust the savings amounts. Consistently applying this practice will improve your finances over time and help you achieve your goals quicker.

I know this has been a long chapter, and thanks for sticking with me till the end.

Summary

Gaining control over your money is key to financial success. Many people who have tried budgeting have given up or failed miserably at the task. Outdated budgeting practices and tracking apps don't work because they're either too demanding or keep your finances constantly at the forefront of your mind – often taking the joy out of living.

An alternative is to set up a Spending Plan that takes care of all the bills and savings upfront and then calculates an amount that can be used to spend as you please. This method offers a guilt-free and budget-free option that helps you control your cash flow while enjoying life.

11

MAKING THE PLAN WORK

The major advantage of calculating your Spending Margin is that you know exactly how much you can afford to spend each month. This way, you don't have to worry about whether you've met your commitments of paying bills and socking away savings. But, how do you operationalize this or make it work?

How do you know when you've hit the limit of your Spending Margin without detailed tracking or, heaven forbid, go back to budgeting? The key will be to separate the money earmarked for bills and savings from the margin we can spend.

Most of us have our pay go to one account, and then we make payments from this account, whether it's an automatic bill, credit or debit card payments or the mortgage. This strategy will not work for our **Plan** because money for fixed expenses and savings is mingled with our spending money. When you can't differentiate between the two, it's harder to know if you can afford something, and easier to fall back into old habits of spending what you don't have.

The Mastermind Banking Plan

A simple but effective banking strategy will help you implement your **Plan** so that you don't spend more than your margin. Here's how it works:

Step 1: Separate the money you should not spend into your primary chequing account

To accomplish this, you will require two chequing accounts. The one in which your pay is deposited will suffice. You will pay your Fixed Expenses, Important, Interim and Retirement Savings from this account. Under no circumstances should it be touched for any other purpose. Think of it as already spent. You can rename this account "Fixed Expenses and Savings" or anything else that you wish that describes its purpose.

1. FIXED EXPENSES and SAVINGS account

In our example of the Wangs, $3,329 made up their fixed expenses ($1,485), Important ($560), Interim ($784) and Retirement Savings ($500). These are to be separated to pay these commitments.

. . .

Step 2: Separate the money you can spend into another chequing account

The second chequing account will be where your "Spending Margin" money goes into. These are the funds that you can use guilt-free, at your will. Ensure that any debit card is attached to this account so that anytime you make ATM withdrawals or debit payments, they come out of this spending account.

When setting up these multiple accounts, ensure you understand the bank fees. You may have to shop around for a low-fee bank account or negotiate with the bank if you have several financial products with them. Nonetheless, even a small charge for having two bank accounts will be worth the cost if you can implement this **Plan**.

For the Wangs, their "Spending Margin" was $1,671, so they would transfer this amount into this account, knowing they could spend every last dollar if they wanted. Again, this account could be named "Spending Margin," "Yahoo Money," or whatever is preferred that describes its purpose.

2. SPENDING MARGIN account

Step 3: Determine how much should be in each account per pay period.

Since this **Plan** works on a monthly cycle, you will want to allocate money to your Spending Margin account based on your pay period (when money is coming in) and the timing of your bill payments, like the mortgage and utility expenses (when money is going out). In assigning the Spending Margin for each pay period, you get away from spikes in your account balance at one point in the month compared to another.

Plan to have any income (pay, investments, spousal

support, other) deposited into your Fixed Expenses and Savings account. Then after each pay period, transfer funds into your Spending Margin account. For instance, the Wang's spending margin is $1,671, and he gets paid twice a month. Therefore, from each paycheque of $2,500, they would transfer $836 from the Fixed Expense and Savings account to the Spending Margin account.

Chen and Jeng are left with $1,664 in the Fixed Expense and Savings Account to pay for these commitments for the first part of the month. With the second pay coming two weeks later, this process will be repeated. Now that the Spending Margin account is replenished every pay period, the Wangs can spend that $836 down to zero if they want. They can go for groceries or out for dinner and know the exact amount in this account.

When using credit cards for purchases, one can easily rack up the expenses, thinking they will pay off the balance next month. One way to prevent that in our **Plan** is to transfer the amount charged to a credit card from your Spending Margin account to the credit card balance every day or couple of days. This has a dual purpose: to give you a real-time balance on how much you have in your Spending account; and mitigate the possibility of you overspending on your credit card.

Step 4: Automate as Much As Possible

Over my lifetime, I've incurred penalties and charges for late bill payments, or the periodic payment not going through because of insufficient funds. The ironic thing is that I had the funds; I just forgot, or I didn't manage my bank account properly. Automated payments have changed all of that. There should be no excuse for these types of fees and penalties in today's financial environment.

Automate all Fixed Expenses, Important and Interim and

Retirement Savings so that you never miss a payment. If the bills can be paid at the end of the month, choose that option so the money stays in your account longer and you make interest. For the savings, especially Retirement or Tax-free savings accounts (TFSA's in some countries), the earlier in the month, the better, so it has a longer time to accumulate returns over the lifetime. More on TFSA's in the Prosper section. This simple strategy will maximize any interest on your money in the bank and increase your returns on the other investments.

12

OK...REAL LIFE NOW

Now that we've learned about how to **Plan** your finances so you can better control your cash flow and move towards a guilt-free spending margin, let's look at a few real-life examples in this chapter.

Addie and Rodney

Addie, 31, Financial Service Sales
Rodney, 40, Security Guard
Married with 2 young kids aged 2 and 5
Annual gross household income: $115,000
Financial Goals: Own a home, purchase rental properties, upgrade their vehicle and establish retirement savings

Mid-2021, Addie attended our Financial Literacy Program and was deeply interested in increasing her financial knowledge for professional and personal reasons. After the Program, she and her husband Rodney wanted further advice on their finances, so we had several one-on-one sessions. They had been renting for several years but were about to move to another city and they had enough funds to purchase an average-priced home in the city they were heading to.

As we discussed their goals, they were also keen on investing in a rental property. Initially, they had a goal of purchasing the rental property within a year. As we discussed the rules in Canada that require a 20% down payment for rentals, they had to move out their goal by 18 months.

It is not uncommon, as you put "numbers to paper" in your **Plan** to test the reasonableness of your goals. It's one thing to be positive and have a great attitude to advance your financial position; it's another to see how you can effectively execute your **Plan**. However, it is much better to adjust your goals and move towards them as this couple did, than not have any at all.

As we crunched out the numbers in the **Plan**, this is how we calculated their Spending Margin:

Pay Frequency	Net Pay	Pays/Month	Monthly After Tax Income	Total Net Annual Pay
Twice per month	$ 4,175	2	$ 8,350	$ 100,200
Monthly	$ 8,350	1	$ 8,350	$ 100,200

Fixed Expenses		
Rent	$ 1,400	
Phone	$ 150	
Cable	$ 15	
Bank Fees	$ 17	
Car Insurance	$ 214	
Total	**$ 1,796**	
Important Savings		
Down payment for rental ($70,000)	$ 2,500	
Down payment for vehicle ($5,000)	$ 600	
Education Fund for Children	$ 450	
Total	**$ 3,550**	
Interim Savings		
Car Repairs ($1500/yr.)	$ 125	
Gifts ($500/yr.)	$ 42	
Emergency fund	$ 300	
Total	**$ 467**	
Retirement savings		
Retirement for both Addie and Rodney	$ 1,500	
Total	**$ 1,500**	
Spending Margin		
Monthly Take-home pay	$ 8,350	$ 8,350
Fixed Expenses	$ 1,796	
Important Savings	$ 3,550	
Interim Savings	$ 467	
Retirement Savings	$ 1,500	
Sub-total		$ 7,313
Spending Margin		**$ 1,037**

First of all, their Fixed expense ratio of 22% is well below the 50-55% maximum a family would want to experience ($1,796 Fixed expenses divided by the take-home pay of $8,350).

They did a great job of keeping the fixed cost structure low, which this will serve them well as they try to reach their longer-term goals.

A large share of their Important Savings is for the Down Payment on the Rental property they want to purchase in a couple of years ($2,500). The other costs in this category are a down payment on a much-needed and upgraded vehicle ($600) for an expanding family. The last one, an Education Fund for their two children ($450), which is a key value for them.

Addie and Rodney started an Emergency Fund ($300) for Interim Savings, and have also allocated some money for Car Maintenance and Gifts. Finally, since they don't have company pension plans, they've set a stretch goal of putting away 13% of their annual income towards retirement savings for both of them.

A Spending Margin of $1,037 provides Addie and Rodney with ample room to take care of groceries and other expenses of a young family. With bills and savings taken care of upfront, they don't have to worry about how they spend this money in their Spending Margin account.

Addie and Rodney finally made that move to another city. The last time I talked to them, they were continuing to work their **Plan**. This new way to control their finances is slowly increasing their net worth while at the same time moving towards their goals.

Sasha and Allan

Sasha, 54, Community Coordinator
Allan, 62, Real Estate Agent
Married with grown children
Annual gross household income: $153,000

Financial Goals: Both retire within 3-5 years, sell their home and live in another country.

Sasha recently attended our Financial Literacy Program to gain a better understanding of how to invest in stocks and real estate. Subsequent to completing the Program, Sasha and her husband Allan came to see for some financial planning. In the next few years, this couple is planning to end their working careers and move into another phase of life. They've been planful with their finances over the years with funds set up in Retirement account (RRSP's –Registered Retirement Savings Plans) and Tax-free Savings Accounts (TFSA's). Both of these types of accounts are allowed by the Canadian government as a way for Canadians to save for retirement and tax shelter their investments. Other countries may have similar plans.

When they retire, Sasha and Allan's plan is to sell their home and use the funds to buy another property in a country with a warmer climate such as Panama, Mexico or some southern USA States. To get them ready for this change, we reviewed their finances and set up a **Plan**.

This is what we came up with for their Spending Margin.

Pay Frequency	Net Pay	Pays/Month	Monthly After Tax Income	Total Annual Net Pay
Monthly (for both)	$ 6,750	1	$ 6,750	$ 81,000

Fixed Expenses:	
Utilities	$ 460
Water	$ 80
Line of Credit Loan	$ 400
Phone	$ 90
Bank Fees	$ 60
Car & house Insurance	$ 450
Life Insurance	$ 129
Property Taxes	$ 330
Car Payment	$ 477
Total	**$ 2,476**

Important Savings	
Home Equity Loan	$ 600
Entertainment	$ 95
Renovations	$ 400
Vacation	$ 600
Total	**$ 1,695**

Interim Savings	
Car Repairs ($600/yr.)	$ 50
Gifts ($1000/yr.)	$ 84
Timeshare Maintenance Cost	$ 84
Total	**$ 218**

Retirement Savings	
Retirement	$ 800
ETF (Exchange Traded Funds)	$ 200
Total	$ 1,000

Monthly Income	$ 6,750	$ 6,750
Fixed Expenses	$ 2,476	
Important Savings	$ 1,695	
Interim Savings	$ 218	
Retirement Savings	$ 1,000	
Sub-total		$ 5,389
Spending Margin		$ 1,361

As we reviewed Sasha and Allan's **Plan**, we determined that the fixed expense ratio was 37%. This is a very healthy number and below the 50-55% maximum someone should have ($2,476 Fixed Expenses divided by the take-home pay of $6,750).

Most of the Important Savings is for a Home Equity Loan ($600) they took out a few years ago (and want to pay off), planned renovations of $400, and a well-deserved vacation fund ($600).

For Interim Savings, they have very few costs. There's been some money set aside for gifts, car repairs and Timeshare maintenance costs totaling ($218) for the three.

Although an Emergency Fund was recommended, Sasha and Allan decided not to start one as they felt they had enough money in their bank accounts and other investments to cover any emergencies that might come up. They made a personal decision based on risk and the probability of an emergency they felt they may encounter.

Concerning Retirement Savings, the couple is putting away about 8% of their gross income into two accounts ($1,000 per month = $12,000 per year. Gross income of $153,000 divided by $12,000). Although this is slightly below the 10% rule-of-thumb, Sasha and Allan are close to retirement and believe they have already saved enough to position them well into the future.

As we get to the final numbers, their Spending Margin of $1,361 is fairly substantial for the couple to spend in a given month. They will use these funds for groceries, gas, household items, personal care and one of Sasha's favorite past times, gardening.

Summary

In this PLAN Section, we've learned an alternate method to traditional budgeting. This simple but effective process is being practiced by many students of our Program and clients wanting to gain control over their finances.

Ok...Real Life Now: Action Step

Now it's your turn. Go to the *Fast Track to Prosperity Workbook* and develop your own Spending Plan. Review the last few chapters. It may take a few hours at first to find the information on past expenses but once the Spending Plan is set up, it will be an easy method to follow from month to month. Take some time also to set up your bank accounts so you can easily track and know how much you have at any time as your Spending Margin.

Finally, don't be discouraged if it's not perfect the first few months. There's always some adjustments that can be made to continuously improve the process. After a few cycles, you will get the hang of it and find that it's actually an easy way manage your money.

The various downloadable charts can be found at
www.fasttrack2prosperity.com/bonus
Or scan this QR code with your phone camera.

Financial Literacy Program, Level 2, June 2017

Financial Literacy Program, Level 1, June 2017

Financial Literacy Program, Level 1, June 2019

SECTION THREE – PROSPER

AFTER DEVELOPING A PLAN, THE ICE CREAM KID FINALLY PROSPERS

My Last Update on Chilly Willy

Last time, you may remember that I came across a large banner about a summer camp. This eventually led me to an excellent opportunity to sell my ice cream. My **PLAN** was in place, and I was about to finally **PROSPER.**

As the summer camp opened in mid-July, I was excited about the prospect of providing cool treats to a litany of young campers. Every morning, I would arrive and park my cart under a big oak tree that provided shade from the scorching sun. And every couple of hours, as there was a break in daily activities, kids would take time out to come and buy ice cream.

Wednesdays were particularly special days of the week for me, though. On this day, at headquarters, I would ask them to "load me up." Yes, this was the day that the summer camp would buy ice cream for each of the 400 campers. To do this properly and efficiently, I would use the camp store to hand out the treat. The line-ups were long, but with the help of a couple of the camp staff, we were able to deliver the frosty delights to the youngsters.

Those days were long and hectic but so much worth the effort. I continued to learn some important lessons that summer. The importance of **PAUSING** to think about my goals and how to achieve them. Then, having a **PLAN** and slowly working that **PLAN**. Goal achievement rarely occurs overnight. As we've seen in the first section of the book under goals, some can be short-term while others may take longer. But the key is "sticking to" the **PLAN** and doing something every day, however small, to eventually achieve the goal.

During those summer months, I earned more money than I had ever made in my short working career. I realized the value of persistence and not giving up. Had I adopted a defeatist attitude after being escorted off that area of the city by my competitors, I may never have come across that camp banner, which led to my ability to **PROSPER**.

13

CREDIT CARD USE...FRIEND OR FOE?

Jenny and Hoquiam came to see me for some help in getting their finances under control. As we calculated their net worth, it was obvious where the main issue resided. Jenny confided how she was able to get a credit card fairly easily after college and used it for all her purchases. The credit card company would continue to increase her limit. Each time the limit increased, she would slowly creep up to that amount, eventually resulting in a high credit card debt.

Hoquiam immigrated to Canada about ten years ago. When he opened up his bank account under a Newcomer Program, they gave him a major credit card with a small limit that increased over time. He stated that he got all caught up in this newfound credit and just started spending because he felt it was the "Canadian" thing to do. Hoquiam and Jenny confessed that they've never paid off the total monthly amount for as long as they've been together. In fact, most of the time, making the minimum payment was the norm. This couple's story is not uncommon these days.

In Chapter 1, The Financial Landscape, I offered an overview of current debt levels and a bit of history around how we got there. In some ways, it was probably easier for our grandparents to stay out of debt, primarily because credit wasn't as readily available. In that generation, they only borrowed for the purchase of a home. The thought of using credit and getting into debt for vacations or other consumer spending was unheard of and went against their core financial values.

But here we are. With record-level low-interest rates in North America and some European countries, consumers have accumulated increasing debt, over the past several years. Americans have the highest number of credit cards per citizen compared with the European Union (EU) and Canada. Americans have an average of four credit cards, and the EU ranges from 0.1 to 3.9 cards per inhabitant.[1] The average for Canadians is in the middle, with an average of two cards for each citizen.[2] Go to any mall, and you'll be accosted by someone in a kiosk asking you to apply for mainstream credit cards. Or worse, they'll try to sign you up for store-branded ones that carry an even higher interest rate. In a store, the cashier may also ask if you want to sign up for their store credit card, at times with incentives such as a credit like $50 off your purchase or that *irresistible travel bag*. However good the deal sounds, having an additional card and the credit associated with it, may be a recipe for getting into further debt if not managed well. Especially if the card is not needed in the first place. The person making you the offer is handsomely compensated if you sign up because they know how valuable an additional credit card in circulation could be for their business.

Most folks hold on to their credit cards for years, making us a precious commodity to credit card companies. However, I don't want to leave the impression that having credit cards leads us to be ensnared into a death trap as if we have no choice in managing them. We have choices, and credit cards have many benefits, when responsibly used.

Moderation is Always a Good Principle

Some financial experts strongly advise against using any credit cards and insist that to control the "debt snare," we should use cash for every purchase. Unfortunately, sometimes these folks are either on one side of the pendulum or the other and think it should be the same for every individual. However, we're not all the same, and one size or strategy doesn't fit for all. I will concede that there may be times when cash is preferable but there is a way to make use of all the BENEFITS of credit cards and know how to manage the potential pitfalls.

In addition, the media loves to play on our emotions and makes us feel that we are all doomed. As stated before, you are **NOT** a victim. You are in control of your finances. Any financial problems are a result of personal choices, which need to be acknowledged, declared and placed in the rearview mirror, so you can move forward in your financial journey.

Here's My Perspective...Boost Your Benefits of Using Credit Cards

Assuming you are not in the category of debt I described above, there are some pretty good benefits to having and using credit cards:

1. **Free short-term loan** – when you make a purchase, you may not have to pay off those purchases for 4-6 weeks, depending on the date in your payment cycle. Having the money in our account for that period of time, earning interest, is better than in the credit company's coffers.
2. **Free warranty extensions** – many credit cards offer instant extended warranty coverage on electronics and appliances, thereby avoiding the costly versions offered by the retailer.
3. **Keeps track of your expenses** – many companies provide a detailed listing of your purchases by major category, or you can download the details for free. This information is invaluable for preparing the Spending Plan (Budget) phase of your finances.
4. **Rewards and points** – often can add up to thousands of dollars worth of services. If you are going to be spending the money anyway, you might as well make use of the freebies.
5. **International travel** – lost or stolen cards can be easily replaced, whereas cash is simply gone.
6. **Price protection** – some credit card companies will refund the difference if you buy something and then find a lower price on the identical product within 90 days.
7. **Free car rental coverage –** you can decline the high, daily car rental company insurance rates if you rent the vehicle on many credit cards. In addition, your personal car insurance should also cover you, so there is no need to purchase the costly one.
8. **Helps establish good credit –** if payments are made on time, one can develop a consistent and

healthy credit score. This will come in handy when applying for a loan or mortgage.

9. **Trip cancellation insurance** – if you book a vacation and can't travel because you get sick, often the airlines will levy some charge. Many credit card companies cover this cost.

The 7 Credit Card Rules

Okay, now that we've reviewed the many benefits of credit cards, I would be remiss if I didn't highlight the cautions. Over the years, I've learned some good, solid rules about managing credit cards. Here they are:

1. **THE MOST IMPORTANT ONE: Pay off your total credit card balance every month**. This is the only way you win with credit card companies. They're betting on you only paying the minimum so they can charge you the APR (Annual Percentage Rate). I always ask my students if they know their APR. You can guess at the response. No one has ever responded that they know the rate.
2. **If you can't pay off the entire balance, DO NOT miss the payment.** Paying at least the minimum amount is better than missing a payment. When you miss a payment, this may affect your credit score negatively. To ensure you never miss a payment, set up an automatic payment for the due date.
3. **Ask to get the annual fees waived on your cards.** Call your credit card company and ask if they can waive the fee for the year, especially if you have been with them for a long time. They don't want to lose your business, and calling them a few weeks before the fee is due is a good time to

negotiate. The worst thing they can do is say no, so you've got a 50% chance.

4. **If you can't pay off your total balance every month, negotiate a lower APR**. When you carry a balance, you pay ridiculously high interest rates and the credit card companies LOVE you. You might as well call them and ask for a reduction. For those who follow Rule #1, there is no need to negotiate a lower APR because you are paying off the balance every month, so no interest is charged to you. CONGRATULATIONS!
5. **Take advantage of all the perks**. Many people get certain cards for the rewards, so since you're paying an annual fee, make sure you get your money's worth. Some of these benefits were just previously explained.
6. **Stay loyal – it will be worth it**. When applying for a loan, lenders favor a long history of credit. It's hard to build that up if you're closing credit cards in one place and opening others in another. Don't fall for all those offers like low APR's and travel bags and, in turn, lose out on the stability factor that affects your credit score.
7. **Limit your credit cards to 2-3**. I've coached people that have over 15 cards. The reason? They were attracted by all the offers – free points, concert tickets, credit off their first purchase, amusement park passes, to name a few. All those offers or incentives are simply a clever marketing scheme used by credit card companies, which hire psychologists and human behaviorists on staff. They are specialists in human behavior and know how we think and the impulse triggers that convince us to buy or take the offer. Once we

understand this, we have a better chance of controlling our credit card debt.

Those who fall for all the incentives now have all this credit available to them. The temptation to spend money on credit is so strong, and almost impossible to withstand. Before they know it, they have so much credit debt that few lenders will lend them any money for a larger purchase like a car or home. Was it worth the "Grand Ferris Wheel" ride with the free amusement park tickets we received when we signed up for that store credit card?

I've found that having 2-3 cards that one keeps active for a long time is the safest bet to demonstrate to lenders your ability to be loyal and credit-worthy.

What to do with extra credit cards over this number? Well, there's a good recipe that I've found that may help. First, call the credit card company and cancel them. Then using scissors, cut them up, place them on a cookie sheet and bake at 400 F (200 C) degrees for 20 min. Finally, let them cool and discard or keep as a reminder of the amount of dangerous credit that you were carrying and how you've overcome it. At times, drastic situations call for drastic measures.

Summary

Over the last fifty years, use of credit cards has made it easier for people to get into debt. However, when appropriately used, credit cards hold many benefits. The key is to understand the potential pitfalls and take advantage of the many benefits to gain that upper hand on credit card companies. Remember, you are in control of your finances!

Credit Card Use...Friend or Foe?: Action Step

Let's turn it over to you now. Go to the *Fast Track to Prosperity Workbook* and do the exercise to determine how well you handle credit. This task will deal with your knowledge of your credit card(s), the advantages and whether you are managing them properly. Finally, there is some free info on scripts to use when dealing with credit card companies and negotiating lower APR's.

These extras can be found at
www.fasttrack2prosperity.com/bonus
Or scan this QR code with your phone camera.

14

CAREFUL: HANDLE DEBT WITH CARE

In the previous chapter, I highlighted the notion that as consumers, we are constantly inundated with aggressive marketing tactics. These companies spend millions telling us we need their products and services. After all, we deserve it. Products are strategically placed in stores so that we act on impulse rather than logic. Surfing online for anything will get you an infinite barrage of popups on items related to your search. Online shopping is effortless. It's no wonder many people admit that their debt slowly crept up on them.

As discussed earlier in this book, poor financial management can often lead to 'money shame.' It's easy for a person to look back and wish they had made different financial decisions. Realizing that accumulated debt is out of control can often lead to a deep sense of money shame and regret.

It is important to remember that there is **ALWAYS** a solution to money problems. Each situation is unique to personal circumstances, and the steps to resolve the issue may be difficult. But there *is* hope. If you feel hopeless, remember to reach out to someone for help and advice. Many countries have rights and protections when it comes to debt. Although money is important, it is NEVER, EVER more valuable than life itself.

Types of Debt

From the Lender's perspective, not all debt is created equal.

> **Secured Debt** – this is debt that is backed up by collateral to reduce the risk associated with lending. If the person defaults on their loan payment, the Lender has the right to seize the asset, sell it and pay off the loan outstanding. The interest rate on secured debt is often lower than unsecured. Examples may include property, a car or company shares.
>
> **Unsecured Debt** – this is money that is not backed up with collateral. If the borrower defaults, there is no recourse for the Lender. It is important to remember that it is up to the Lender to determine if they require collateral or not. If they don't, they take on a higher risk and may charge a higher interest for the loan. The

most common types of unsecured debt are credit card debt and student loans.

Debt...and...More Debt

Directionally speaking, we should be striving for as little debt as possible. Anytime we pay interest, that money is 'gone' and can't be used for other purposes such as lifestyle choices or investments. However, it's understandable that it may not be possible to save enough money to make large purchases like a home or car. In those cases, at least the down payment should be as large as possible to reduce the amount of interest paid over the life of the loan.

Many people classify debt as "good" or "bad." How debt is classified depends on whether the debt incurred will help you generate future income (student loan, small business loans) or if the asset purchased appreciates over time (house). Examples of bad debt would include loans or debt used for consumable purchases (travel, clothing, payday loans) or assets that depreciate over time (sports and recreational equipment.)

Again, the intent here is not to lay on some guilt because you have more bad than good debt, but rather get you to think about debt before making the commitment.

Jay and Shuhra arrived at the café we were meeting at with a stack of papers in hand. As we discussed their situation, they told me about the payday loan they had outstanding for several months. This type of loan is provided by companies that prey on individuals with financial challenges and are looking for a quick loan to make ends meet. Typically, it helps someone until their next paycheque. The interest rate one payday loans is ridiculously high.

The young couple finally got to rent a new apartment, and to furnish the unit, they bought some new furniture through several Rent-to-Own loans. Again, the interest rate is high in these arrangements, and the terms favor the lender. If one fails to make a payment, they can take away the furniture or appliances and you are left with nothing.

We PAUSED to discuss their situation and then put a PLAN in place to get them out of these "bad debts." Knowing about this type of credit helped them, but it was still a painful lesson for them in poor credit management. They left our meeting with a renewed sense of hope.

Four Rules for Reducing Debt

1. Identify Your Debt

The first step in getting control over debt is to KNOW how much debt you have. You'll remember that when I asked my students if they knew the APR (Annual Percentage Rate) on their credit cards, they didn't know, and I believed them. Suppose I asked the same question about debt without asking for some proof through statements and documents. There is no way to know if they're telling me the truth or if they know for sure what their debt levels are.

According to a recent study, some people seriously underestimate their debt when it comes to credit cards and loans. Comparing what American consumers reported as debt and what is actually owed to lenders was off by 40%.[1] This is not a rounding error! Debt consisting of mortgages, Lines of Credit and car loans lined up fairly close, but there was a significant gap between the two reported numbers when it came to credit card and student loans.

In Chapter 7, in determining your net worth, we reviewed how to calculate your liabilities (debt). Now, you can make a list of all the debt you owe. Identify the interest rate on each one and the minimum monthly payment. Finally, decide what new payment you will make going forward. This will all depend on how "aggressively" you want to eliminate the debt and MUST be much HIGHER than the minimum payment. (See number 4 below)

Listing of Debts I Owe				
Name of Debt	**Total amount of Debt**	**APR**	**Minimum Monthly Payment**	**New Payment**
Credit Card- VISA	$3,400	22%	$250	$500
Mortgage – Bank of the Alps	$100,000	5%	$1,000	$1,250
Student Loan	$5,000	1%	$300	$400
Total	**$108,400**		**$1,550**	**$2,150**

2. Prioritize Your Debt

The reason for identifying the debt and the interest rate associated with each one is that it will help you prioritize which debt to pay first. Obviously, the higher the APR, the more it is costing you to carry that debt. There are several methods for deciding what to pay first. There are advantages to each one. Rather than get into a lengthy debate about which one is better, I will list the various methods, and you can choose the method that best suits you.

Prioritizing Your Debt			
Strategy	Traditional Method	Snowball Method	Emotional Method
How it works	Rank your debts by interest rate - highest to lowest. Pay the minimum on all the debts and then pay off the one with the highest interest rate. Repeat with the next highest one.	Rank your debts by amount owing -lowest to highest. Pay the minimum on all debts and then pay off the one with the lowest dollar value. Repeat with the next one on the list	Rank your debts by the ones that bother you the most. Pay the minimum on all debts and then pay off the next one on the list.
Why it works	From a financial perspective, the debt costing you the most should be paid off first	Psychologically, it's powerful to get a small win and this can be motivation to pay off the next one.	This one is more about "peace of mind." Sometimes, we have those debts that cause us stress or "nag" us. Again, psychologically, it's a good idea to get them off the list

3. Call Your Lenders and Negotiate a Lower Interest Rate

We're not used to asking for a "break" on fees, but most Lenders would rather get some of their loan repaid than take a risk that you are not able to pay back any of it. They certainly don't want to send it to Collection Agencies. A Lender will use a Collection Agency after several attempts to get their loan repaid without success. This has an administration fee the Lender must pay, plus the Collection Agency also takes a handsome fee for service.

Therefore, if you call a Lender and ask them for a lower rate, you have a 50% chance of getting it changed. You have nothing to lose except lower interest costs over the life of the loan.

Jason C. attended the Financial Literacy Program lesson on Credit where we reviewed the rules for reducing debt. A month later, he shared in class how he called his credit card company and was able to lower his APR from 22% to 16%. Jason said that this simple action would reduce his total interest on the loan by $800.

4. Use Newfound Savings to Further Reduce Debt

Now that you know how to "PLAN" (Section 2) better and have more control over your finances, you should be able to find some extra money. What do you do with this extra cash? Aggressively apply it to your debt by making much larger payments than the minimum required by the Credit Card Company, financial institution or lender.

Later in this PROSPER section, we will also look for additional ways to save money. If you have debt, don't just spend any newfound savings frivolously. Get serious about debt and make a conscious effort to reduce it. It may mean that you set up automatic transfers that go directly to paying off a specific debt. It may mean a family meeting is necessary to ensure everyone is on board towards the goal. This is not easy! And will seem difficult at first, but after you get into the habit of reducing debt, you will experience "wins," which will motivate you to continue.

We live in times where we really believe that being in debt, especially consumer debt, is normal. Change this mindset and get serious about purposely and aggressively reducing it to ZERO.

Imagine all the other uses for your money if it wasn't tied up in debt. Examples of this are investments with future growth potential, extras for yourself or your family, or supporting your lifestyle and financial goals.

Summary

If there is one element of your finances that can create havoc and get you totally off-track of your financial and lifestyle goals...it is debt. Accumulated debt means you are paying off a financial commitment made in the past but with an added cost of interest. This additional interest cost "eats" into the excess money you could otherwise use to invest in assets that will provide you with future consumption.

We reviewed some general rules for reducing debt. This includes knowing how much debt you have and prioritizing your debt, so you have a definite plan to reduce it. Some like to rank their debt according to the interest rate, while others choose to do it by its amount or emotional value. Everyone is different. If you require the psychological boost of the last two methods, then choose that but remember that it will cost you more. The simple math is that the higher the interest rates on your debt, the more you will pay overtime.

Nonetheless, get serious about debt reduction. It will be challenging at times, especially if one is in a lot of debt. It may mean going about life with less while seeing your friends and families spend and do things you wish you could. But prevail; it will be worth it. Debt issues have a tendency to creep into other areas of our lives, including our relationships, and mental and physical wellness. Do yourself a favor and eliminate debt. It is a critical step towards financial success and achievable with a reasonable plan and heartfelt desire.

Careful: Handle Debt with Care: Action Steps

Here's some action you can take. Go to the *Fast Track to*

Prosperity Workbook and do the exercise that lists your debts like the one in this chapter. Then determine which method you will use to pay off your loans: Traditional, Snowball or Emotional.

Finally call any Lenders to negotiate a lower APR as appropriate. You may be surprised how some of them may lower the payment, APR or length of the term.

The debt chart can be found at
www.fasttrack2prosperity.com/bonus
Or scan this QR code with your phone camera.

15

THE PATH TO INVESTING

The main reason for developing Level 2 of the Financial Literacy Program (FLP) was the overwhelming feedback we received about picking stocks for investments. It seems to be a very popular subject. After all, investments are one of the best ways to build a financial reserve for the future.

However, many people feel they are either not appropriately prepared to start investing in the stock market or want to improve their methods. There is a multitude of books, courses and information on how to invest in stocks. The sheer number of resources can be daunting to the new investor. I spend several lessons in the FLP teaching the *"Prospero"* method of investing but won't be going into detail here. Perhaps I'll delve into this more thoroughly in a future project, but it is not the intent of this book. However, I want to review a few principles about investing in the market.

To begin with, the best way to make money in the stock market is to own and hold securities that make interest, dividends, and capital gains over the long-term. **PLEASE reread that statement**. This is a long term process that can lead to significant gains with patience and consistent returns. It is not rapid or impulsive trading. I've found that many novice investors jump in and out of the market based on a casual stock tip or of their own personal whims. This is not the way to grow your investment over the long term if you're constantly trying to chase returns and being emotionally swayed by the "ups and downs" of the market.

In fact, just last month, I was discussing investing and huge swings in the market over the last few years with a friend of mine, whose net worth is well over five million dollars. His exact comment to me was, "Jay, I've always kept it simple, just invest in high quality securities and let it grow."

In previous chapters, we discussed how when you borrow money, whether on a loan or on credit and, if it is not paid before the end of the billing cycle, you pay interest to the lender or creditor. This takes money out of your pocket, which could otherwise be used for other purposes like long-term investing.

You go to any bookstore or search online, and there are piles of information on how to invest and pick stocks. Each writer champions their method like the latest car models on the first day of an International Auto Show. "If you just do this"; "just follow these six easy steps"...and so on, and so forth.

The truth is, is that there is NO fail-proof or infallible strategy that will guarantee success. I always begin this lesson in the FLP by telling my students that if they're looking for the magic key or prescription to picking stocks... they will be sorely disappointed! Why? The reasons can be summed up as follows:

- there are so many factors and variables that affect a company's health that it is impossible to construct a formula for success
- a lot of information is intangible – qualitative characteristics like management, company staff, reputation, etc. and, of course,
- the human (often irrational) element that affects the stock market

Not all Income is Treated Equal

One concept often overlooked by investors is how the income they generate from their investments will be taxed. Individual countries will have different tax laws and rates for your returns on investments. For instance, if you own bonds, your return on this investment is considered interest income and duly taxed in many jurisdictions.

Dividends are payments of profits made to investors who own a company's stock. Depending on the country, this type of income may be treated more favourably for tax purposes. You may pay less income tax for a dollar of dividend income versus a dollar of employment or interest income.

Finally, capital gains are the profits from the sale of a share or stock in a company. It's the fruits of your labour for investing and holding onto this type of asset. Again, the rules on how this profit is taxed may vary between different countries. Similar to dividends, they are usually taxed lower than interest income.

The tax treatment on capital gains and dividends is more favourable because governments want us to fuel the economy by investing in it. In Canada, dividend income from eligible Canadian corporations is taxed even lower than other types of dividend income to encourage investment in Canadian corporations.

	Types Of Investment Income		
	Interest Income from Bonds	Dividend Income	Capital Gains
Tax Treatment	Taxed – HIGH	Taxed – Low to Med	Taxed – Low to Med

A quick review of the rate your income is taxed is important in choosing the type of investment strategy you should have. This is quickly done by searching online for the tax rate on the three types of investment income in your country, province, state or jurisdiction.

For instance, at the time of this writing, interest rates in Canada and the U.S. are historically low. Yet, interest income is taxed at a higher rate than dividend and capital gains. So, investing in bonds or having a lot of money in cash at the bank (without a good reason), makes you the least amount of interest. It is also being taxed at the higher rate. Take into account inflation, and you're potentially losing money (also referred to as losing purchasing power.)

Jumping into any investment without a proper grounding is unwise. Therefore, I'd like to offer several steps in preparation before investing.

Steps in Preparation to Invest

1. **You have a surplus left over to invest after meeting your financial obligations.** After implementing the PLAN section of the book, you either have some extra funds in your spending margin or have explicitly saved for investing.
2. **Ensure your Emergency Fund requirements are met.** As reviewed in the previous section, have 3-9 months of reserve in this account.
3. **Review your Core Values around risk tolerance.** Investing always includes some risk; therefore, it's important to determine what level of risk you are prepared to take when getting into the stock market.
4. **Set realistic expectations for your returns**. We often hear about individuals who invested in Apple, Netflix or Amazon when they were a few dollars and then made "millions." However, we rarely learn about those who lost their entire investment in another company. Ensure you establish a reasonable rate of return for your investments to avoid disappointment and a drop in your future pool of funds.
5. **Do your due diligence.** Do your homework and understand the probabilities of success and failure with any investment. Nothing takes the place of using a process where you collect and analyze available information before making an investment.
6. **Diversify your Investments.** Mitigate your potential losses by spreading the risk across different types of investments. This includes

various industries, company size and type amongst, others.

Investment Pyramid Options

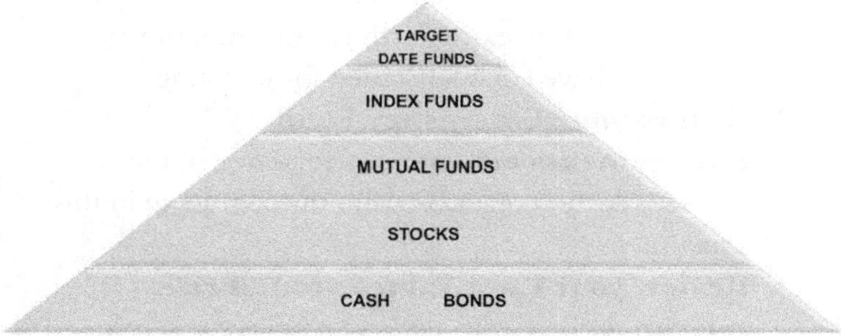

The chart above shows the various choices one has for investments. At the bottom, there are Cash and Bonds. Cash is simply money on hand that's not invested. Cash is the safest part of your assets, but it also earns the lowest reward. You will want to have some cash for your emergency fund (reviewed in the previous section on "PLAN.")

Bonds offer a promise to pay your original investment plus an interest component. The interest rate paid is usually higher than simply keeping money in the bank, but you don't have access to your funds until the bond matures (when it is due to you). A further advantage of bonds is that they are typically a safe investment, and they reduce your portfolio's risk.

In the following section, we will review the remainder of the investment options.

How to Invest in the Stock Market

Now that you have considered the steps in preparing to invest, it's time to decide **HOW** you will do this. There are several options available to you. Let's review them:

1. Buy and sell individual stocks: Great if you have the time and knowledge, but risky.

With this option, you open a trading account, and you buy and sell individual companies shares. A trading account can be opened with a brokerage firm with several options available to you:

Type	Characteristics	Examples
Full service brokers	• Offer a large amount of financial products and services including advice on when to buy and sell • Provide access to research and in-depth information on a particular company • Charge a fee that may be based on volume purchased and share price • Since representatives of these type of firms receive commissions on their sales, ensure that any recommendations fit your financial Core Values and risk profile	Merrill Lynch, Morgan Stanley, Kotak Securities, Laurentian Bank of Canada
Discount brokers	• Charge a reduced, flat fee per trade • Do not offer financial advice on trades • Provide support on how to place a trade • May place trade either online or by person	CIBC Investor's Edge, Questtrade
Online-only brokers	• Charge a low flat fee per trade or $0. The lowest fee of all brokers • Do not offer financial advice on trades and may offer information through robo-support • Place trade online	Wealth Simple, E*Trade,

Someone asked Warren Buffet how to become a better investor. Pointing to a stack of annual reports, he said, "Read 500 pages like this every day. That's how knowledge works. It builds up like compound interest. All of you can do it, but I guarantee not many of you will do it."[1]

You'll probably agree that most of us do not have the time, patience or "ice-in-our-veins" to be like Warren Buffet. So let's not kid ourselves. That is one of the issues with buying and selling individual stocks. One needs to be prepared to invest time in acquiring or buying the knowledge (through online experts, newsletters, etc.) to make sound decisions. Even then, one is taking a considerable risk.

But Jay, isn't every investment a risk? Of course, but when trying to buy and sell individual stocks, one takes on "an extra heaping spoonful of risk." Why? For starters, when purchasing a single company stock, even after doing your due diligence, you are not diversified. This means that anything can happen to that company, and if it does, it will impact your investment – good or bad.

A great example is SAAB motors, a mammoth auto manufacturer that started production in 1949 and then went defunct in 2011. Who would have thought that a long-standing car company would go broke? But, if you were invested in SAAB, you would have lost your entire investment in the company.

According to a Yale University study, the average lifespan of a company listed on the S&P 500 Index of leading US companies has decreased by 50 years in the last century. It's gone from 67 years in the 1920s to just 15 years today.[2] This means that even some of the largest corporations in the world are not immune to going out of business, hence, the risk to investments in individual companies.

Advantages of Trading Individual Stocks on your own:

- You can tailor your portfolio (number and type of stocks) as you wish
- Lower overall fees
- You will gain experience in making selections

Disadvantages of Trading Individual Stocks on your own:

- Increased risk
- Less or no diversification
- Lack of 'expert' advice and experience with market trends

2. Mutual funds: Convenient but costly...Watch out!

The mutual fund industry has been around for close to 100 years. It was created to meet the need of investors to have someone 'actively' manage their investments. Most people don't have the time or knowledge to invest wisely and monitor their investments, so the mutual fund manager role was born. Investors are charged a management fee in exchange for this so-called expertise and service. That sounds like a great deal, right? Well, let's hold on and get a better understanding of this proposition.

Simply put, a mutual fund is an investment where investors pool their money and professional fund managers invest the funds on your behalf. It allows the average investor to participate in a basket of companies rather than buy individual stocks independently. This element of diversification is attractive with this option.

Today, there are mutual funds for every company size (known as small, medium or large cap), industry and geographical region worldwide. There is no shortage of choice for us to consider.

With this simple model, Mutual Funds have become a very popular way to invest over the years. They have also been highly profitable and lucrative for financial companies and institutions that offer them. Go to any bank today, and one of the most common financial products they will try to sell you is a mutual fund. Why?

Well, it's the HIGH management fees that are charged for taking care of your investments. That's why. These fees, known as expense ratios, are applied to your funds and just "drain" your returns. The worst part of this deal is that these (did I say) HIGH fees are levied onto your account, regardless of whether they make returns for you or not. Doesn't seem fair at all! It's one thing to pay a hefty charge for great returns, but when they perform poorly…they still get paid! What kind of system is that?

Advantages of Mutual Funds:

- Professionally managed
- Diversification of portfolio - if one company fails, you don't lose your entire investment, and could still prosper if the other investments do really well
- Convenient for the average investor
- Highly regulated by Security Exchange Commissions (SECs) in most countries
- Record keeping – a record of transactions and any applicable taxable portions completed for you

Disadvantages of Mutual Funds:

- **HIGH FEES, HIGH FEES…**This can add up to thousands of dollars or more over the lifetime of your investment.
- **No tailor-made portfolio** – If you want to invest in Apple and General Motors, and your mutual fund does not invest in those companies, they will not be in your portfolio. Even if they are included, the diversified fund will likely have another wide assortment of companies you may not have picked on your own.

In this day and age, even though mutual funds are very popular and convenient, the **HIGH** expense ratios make this not the best choice for investors.

3. Index Funds: The "carefree" person's answer

I've referred to Warren Buffet, one of the world's best investors, several times in the book. Would you take his advice if he gave it to you? I know I would, and most people would do the same. A few years ago, Buffet published a letter to his daughter and two sons about how he thought they should invest when he was no longer around. His recommendation?

"A very low-cost S&P 500 index fund."

Wow, that's it? You mean, don't try to gain knowledge about companies and buy individual stocks?

Yup, that's what he told his kids. Index funds have been around since the mid-seventies, and the premise is that these funds invest in stocks that match the market. So, really they are matching a particular index, like the S&P 500 or some other index. Therefore, if that Index goes up, the Index Fund goes up and vice versa. This is in contrast to mutual funds, where fund managers buy and sell stocks and TRY to beat the market. Again, think of Mutual Funds being "actively managed" and Index funds as "passively managed" because they are simply following a set of parameters.

Mutual Funds promote their performance using specific periods or stats to make their case look better. On the other hand, Index funds make no such claims about beating the market. With Index funds, a computer program tries to match a particular index, resulting in very low costs compared to Mutual Funds. There is also a wide range of Index Funds to choose from: A few examples are U.S. and Asia-Pacific, Oil and Gas and Consumer Product funds. So, the argument is that since the market has always gone up, over the long term, Index Funds offer the investor better performance without the exorbitant fees.

Advantages of Index Funds:

- Low cost

- Easy and convenient to purchase
- More tax-efficient than mutual funds
- Hey, a Warren Buffet recommendation to his kids

Disadvantages of Index Funds:

- **Asset allocation may be misaligned** – Unless you invest in multiple Index Funds, you may not get the proper asset allocation for your financial goals. See the next section for an explanation of asset allocation. This will involve looking at your index funds every 12 – 18 months and rebalancing them if necessary to achieve an appropriate asset allocation. Although this should be done, this is not considered "actively" managing these funds since you are not doing this frequently, such as daily or weekly.

Asset Allocation: A Crucial Element Often Overlooked By Investors

Hopefully, in the previous section, I made a case for the importance of investment portfolio diversification. However, if someone just purchased different stocks or funds with different stocks, they would be diversified, but only within stocks (also known as equities.). That's like an athletic 16-year-old boy being the star player on a kindergarten football team…no competition!

While it's important to diversify amongst stocks, it's just as imperative to diversify across asset classes (stocks, bonds and cash). Too much or not enough in each class is equally risky and can prove fatal to your investments. How assets are allocated could be one of the most crucial investment decisions investors can make. It could mean the difference between having thousands or even hundreds of thousands of dollars in your investments over your lifetime.

There are two variables to seriously consider in asset allocation – age and risk. Every time we have a recession or a downturn in the economy, we hear about older folks who can't retire now because they've just lost a sizeable portion of their funds they were planning to use in their retirement. The more important question is, "Why weren't they appropriately allocated within the asset classes?" They obviously took a higher risk of having more money invested in the market than bonds (fixed income) and cash. Many times, it's a risk that they were unaware of.

Individuals in their twenties and thirties should have a higher percentage in equities and not be as concerned about the risk because of the longer time span before retiring. They will likely go through many ups and downs throughout their lifetime, but they're in it for the long term, so there is no need to fret. However, those that are approaching retirement should reduce their risk by reallocating some of their assets away from equities into less risky ones.

Of course, it's not as simple as saying, "you need to be at one end of the spectrum versus the other for the different age groups." Depending on your personal financial situation and other assets, the rate at which you move into bonds as you age, needs to be considered.

There are different ways to determine your asset allocation based on age. Studies show that we are living longer due to medical advancements and general care for our health. This means that a person could live 20 to 30 years beyond retirement. And even though I believe the fear of running out of money in retirement is overblown, one still needs to ensure there is a good mix of equities to sustain good returns in those latter years.

An Example of Asset Allocation: Based on Age – Modern New Life Model

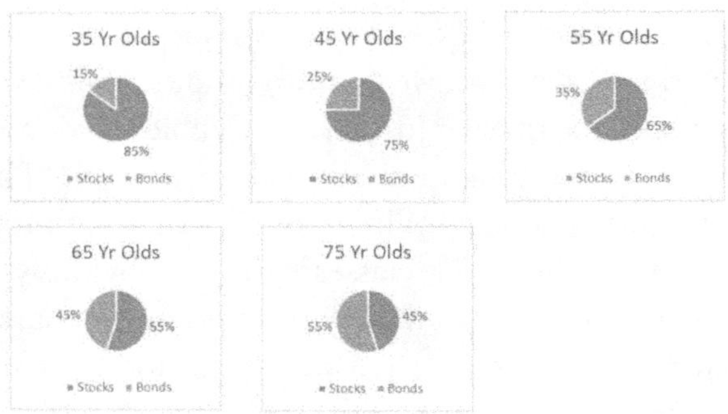

Gerry and Melody, 52 and 49, came to see for some money coaching, and we discussed the concept of asset allocation. After some information gathering, their profile could be classified as a "Modern New Life" couple and looks something like this:

- Due to family medical history and healthy lifestyles, they plan to live well into their early eighties
- Don't have an interest in actively managing their investments but will rely mainly on these assets to live in retirement
- Plan to retire at age 65, plus or minus 3 years
- Plan to remain physically and mentally active into their retirement

Several months after we met, Gerry called me to say that they felt a "huge weight lifted off their shoulders" after our meeting. He said they were really concerned about how much money they needed, and whether they had enough to last their retirement. After discussing the asset allocation concept, they believed they had a solid plan for the future.

Again, every situation needs to be viewed in light of total assets, financial and lifestyle goals, health and other personal variables. However, do you see how understanding asset allocation is so valuable? You've worked hard or are working hard at saving for retirement, DO NOT neglect one of the most critical investment choices – ASSET ALLOCATION.

4. TARGET DATE FUNDS: AN EASY WAY TO INVEST

Have you ever heard of the 80/20 rule? It's a concept about the imbalance between inputs and outputs. In other words, if you try to achieve 100% of a solution, it doesn't guarantee 100% results. Here are some examples you may have heard about:

- 20% of the sales reps generate 80% of total sales
- 20% of employees cause 80% of the problems at work
- And if you've ever worked on most teams, you'll quickly realize that 20% of the people do 80% of the work

So, think of target date funds as representing the 80/20 Rule. They are not perfect, but they "hit" most of the areas of concern we've reviewed thus far. We just discussed the importance of Asset Allocation, Target date funds automatically rebalance your investments based on a retirement date.

For instance, if you turn 65 in 2050 the target date fund may have a name like "ABC Fund 2050," and have more of our money invested in equities. It acts as a sliding scale and slowly moves your investment from equities to bonds (fixed income) as you get older.

Advantages of Target Date Funds:

- Easy and convenient to invest
- Automatically diversify your investments

Disadvantages of Target Date Funds:

- Designed and based on one variable – your retirement age
- Still need to be conscious of management fees

Summary

Investing in the market is one of the best ways to increase the value of your assets. However, to do this, one must adopt a long-term approach, or time horizon, to investing. Before even taking the "plunge" into the market, individuals should determine if they are prepared to invest. Ensuring you follow or, at the very least, consider these steps will help you as you move into the market.

Not all income we receive from investments is taxed the same. A basic understanding of how income is taxed should help determine the investment income that is more advantageous to you.

There are various investment options one can use to build up your financial assets. These make up the Investment pyramid. We discussed the advantages and disadvantages of someone picking their own stocks, mutual funds, index funds and target date funds. Finally, we reviewed the importance of asset allocation as we get closer to retirement.

The Path to Investing: Action Steps

1. Review the 6 Steps in Preparation to investment.
2. Determine which of the four investment options fit your knowledge base, financial core values, risk profile and goals. Some may choose only one, and others a combination of the four…but remember Warren Buffet's advice to his children.
3. If you are going to select your own stocks, determine how you will purchase them (discount, full service, etc.).
4. If you have mutual funds, review the returns over the last several years and be mindful of the high management fees you are paying. Is it time to move to another option like Index or Target Date funds?
5. If you are invested in Index funds when was the last time you rebalanced your portfolio based on asset classes?
6. Review your asset classes in light of your current age and personal financial position. Do you need to rebalance between level of equities and fixed income?

16

GO ALL OUT ON TAX-ADVANTAGED INVESTMENTS

Tax Freedom Day...Time to Celebrate or Maybe Not?

In the early part of the book, I described how governments worldwide are failing to provide leadership around fiscal responsibility. They spend like it's not their money.... Wait...it's not their money; it's ours. And the only way they can fund their spending sprees is to tax its citizens.

I'm always amazed at the concept called Tax Freedom Day. This is the day in the year that the average family has earned enough money to pay the taxes imposed on it. And although various nations report this information, it may not be comparable from one country to another due to the different ways the data is collected. Nonetheless, here are some interesting stats to note.

As you can see, in many countries, the average citizen is working from 29%-59% of the year (Australia and Belgium respectively) to pay all the taxes before earning money for themselves. Therefore, any time the government allows us to reduce that "tax bill," we need to carefully consider the tax advantage available to us.

TAX FREEDOM DAY

Country	Date of Year	Day of Year	Year Updated	Source
Australia	17-Apr	107	2019	Centre for Independent Studies
United States	24-Apr	114	2015	Tax Foundation
New Zealand	7-May	127	2018	Staples Rodway
Uruguay	13-May	133	2010	CPA Ferrere
South Africa	22-May	141	2014	Free Market Foundation
Brazil	31-May	151	2014	Instituto Brasileiro de Planejamento Tributario
Italy	2-Jun	153	2018	CGIA
United Kingdom	12-Jun	162	2017	Adam Smith Institute
Canada	14-Jun	164	2019	Fraser Institute
Spain	30-Jun	181	2016	Foundation for the Advancement of Liberty and Spanish Taxpayer's Union
Germany	11-Jul	192	2015	Bund der Steuerzahler
Israel	14-Jul	197	2013	Jerusalem Institute for Market Studies
France	27-Jul	208	2018	Institut Economique Molinari (IEM)
Belgium	17-Jul	218	2018	Institut Economique Molinari (IEM)

Note Specific References on this chart can be found at the end of the book*

"Next to being shot at and missed, nothing is really quite as satisfying as an income Tax refund."
—F.J. Raymond

Tax Incentives in Various Countries

One area where countries provide tax incentives is for retirement savings. This serves a dual purpose. Firstly, it places less strain on the government to provide pension benefits for its citizens. This means tax revenues can go to support other types of government-sponsored programs. Secondly, it puts some responsibility on the individual to fund their retirement…which is where it belongs.

Traditionally, income and earnings are taxed. Individuals then make contributions with after-tax (T) earnings to Retirement Plans. As you can appreciate, different countries have different incentives to encourage retirement savings. For instance, in some countries, the investment income generated and accumulating in the Retirement Plans is taxed (T) while withdrawals are exempt (E) from taxation. This is generally referred to as the "Taxed-Taxed-Exempt" or "TTE" tax regime.

Many other countries offer an "Exempt-Exempt-Taxed" ("EET") tax regime to retirement savings. In these cases, contributions are exempt (E), and investment returns are also exempt (E) from taxation. In contrast, retirement benefits are treated as taxable (T) income upon withdrawal. This setup is used in Canada, the United States and many European countries.

And then, there are a host of other combinations of the Exemption and Taxes as per the chart below. Check the diagram to confirm the particular situation you are governed by.

The tax treatment of contributions to private pension plans may change according to the source of the contribution (the individual or the employer), their mandatory or voluntary nature, and the type of plan in which they are paid (personal or group plans). It is important to understand the differences in your tax regime, as this ultimately affects the amount of tax you will pay during your retirement plan's accumulation and withdrawal phases.

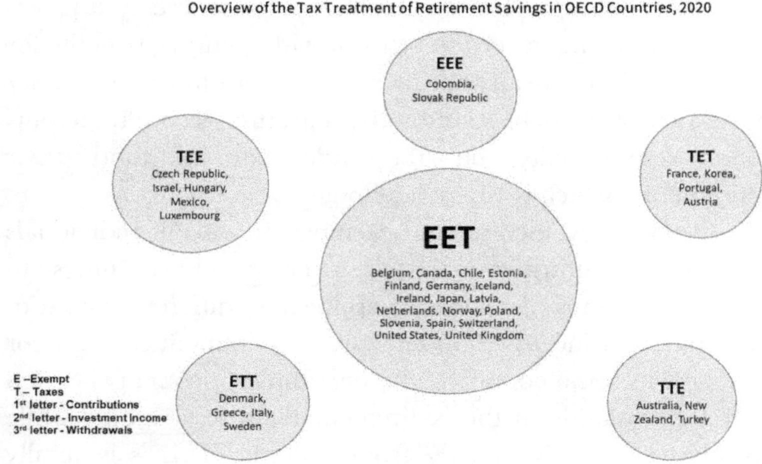

Priorities in Saving for Retirement

As we saw in the "**PLAN**" part of the book, saving for retirement can be a daunting task, especially if we don't make a conscious effort to do it. If the only plan is to use surplus money that's left over at the end of the month, what happens if there's no surplus that month? Exactly… it may never get into that Retirement account. Therefore, to ensure we have funds to enjoy in those later years of life, we need to understand some basic principles and take several necessary steps to help us get there.

Following are some principles that will help you build a solid foundation for retirement. Again, these are general principles that should apply to most situations, regardless of what country you are in.

Principle 1: Start as Young as Possible

We have numerous young people attend our Financial Literacy Program. When I talk about retirement, many don't believe it's a priority in their lives at the moment. After all, it could be decades away, and they're more interested in learning about picking stocks or buying real estate. The truth is that the earlier one starts saving for retirement, the better. The reason? Compound interest. Albert Einstein reportedly described compound interest as the "eighth wonder of the world."

Compound interest means that when you invest money early in life and reinvest your profits over a long period of time, even the smallest amounts can accumulate and grow exponentially to a handsome nest egg.

In the diagram below, let's assume Cindy starts investing $100 a month at age 25 for 40 years to save for retirement and gets a reasonable annual rate of return of 7%. By age 65, she will have approximately $267,000. If Cindy decides to start at 35 years instead, she'll have to more than double her monthly contribution to $216 to accumulate the same amount. She waits another 10 years and starts investing at 45, and it goes up to over $500 a month. So as you can see, the earlier, the better because other expenses will just start showing up in life like mortgages, children and additional associated costs.

If you are older, don't despair. Remember, there is NO MONEY SHAME here. It's never too late to make some changes in your financial affairs. Just make adjustments to your spending plan and invest accordingly for your retirement.

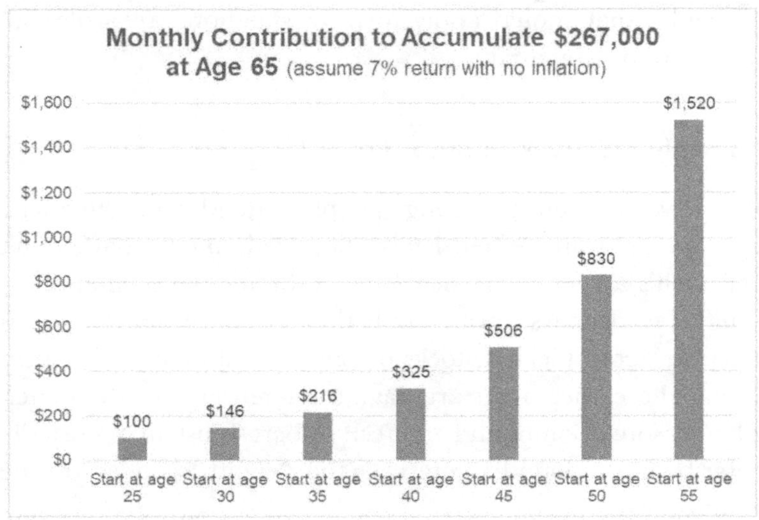

Principle 2: Use Pre-Tax-Dollars Whenever Possible

If possible, using pre-tax dollars to fund your retirement is always a better deal. Since the money you are investing isn't taxed, it means that you have more funds in your account that have the potential to grow by the magic of compounding. Depending on the country and your personal tax rate, this could mean an additional 25 to 40 percent to work with.

When you open up a traditional investment account, you are using after-tax dollars to fund it. For instance, for every $100 you earn (assuming a 25% tax rate), you are now left with $75 to use for investing. Many countries and companies allow you to open a Retirement account with pre-tax dollars. Therefore, your $100 versus $75 a month is used to invest and generate income over decades. This makes a material difference in how much can accumulate in your retirement account.

A simple example illustrates this basic concept. As you can see from the diagram below, the difference between using pre and after-tax money invested at age 20 for 45 years is an astounding \$96,000 or 33%. The extra 25 percent that you can use in your account translates into a significant difference as it compounds over the years.

Investing After-Tax vs. Pre-tax Dollars at age 20		
Amount Invested (monthly)	\$75	\$100
Total Accumulated	\$290,032	\$386,198
(Assuming investment period is 45 years and a 7% rate of return – no inflation)		

Defined Contribution Plans – A Tax-Advantaged Retirement Account

Example 401(k) (United States)

A defined contribution (DC) plan is a common workplace retirement plan in which the employer and the employee contribute money, and the employer makes some form of a matching contribution. In this type of pension plan, you know how much is going into the plan but not how much you will get when you retire because it is based on how well your investment does over time.

In the United States, you wouldn't know what it is by just looking at its name…it's called a 401(k). It is typically set up when an employee first joins a company. There are significant tax advantages as long as you do not withdraw your money from the account until you reach the minimum age of 59½.

Tax Advantages

1. The use of pre-tax dollars to fund your retirement

2. The money that accumulates in the account is not taxed until you withdraw it in retirement and likely to be in a lower tax bracket.

You decide the level of contributions you will make. The employer deducts it from your gross pay (plus the employer portion, if applicable) and remits it to your 401 (k). The funds are then invested in different options, which you would choose and they accumulate over time. See the Path to Investing chapter if you need a refresher.

In Canada, a similar setup is called a defined contribution (DC) plan and works essentially the same way. The only difference is that the minimum age to start withdrawing the funds from the account is 55 years.

Principle 3: Never, Ever Miss an Employer Match

As described above, many companies that offer a defined contribution plan will also match all or part of your contribution. You're probably thinking, "Come on, Jay… there are other priorities like paying down debt, starting an emergency fund or saving for a down payment for a house. I can't do everything." Yeah, I hear you, but a match is **FREE MONEY**. If I came to you and said, "I'd like to give you $100 a month, no strings attached. All you have to do is accept it." Would you take it? I'm thinking most would jump at that proposal.

The way it works is that you have to agree to take the first step in making the contribution before the company matches their portion. Typically, the match is 3 to 6 percent of your annual earnings. Let's look at how important getting this FREE MONEY (Did we say FREE MONEY?) can make to your retirement account.

In this example, an employee starts with a company at age 30, earns $50,000 per year and can contribute up to 5% of their salary, which is matched by the company. The investment generates a modest 7% return and, to keep it simple, I've assumed no salary increases.

The Power of "The MATCH'		
Age	**Balance Without Employer Match**	**Balance With Employer Match**
30	$2,788	$5,469
35	$15,629	$31,117
40	$37,644	$75,087
45	$68,855	$137,424
50	$113,101	$225,797
55	$175,827	$351,081
60	$264,754	$528,695
65	$390,823	$780,494

As you can easily figure out, there is double the money in the account. All the employee did was decide to participate in the DC plan offered by their company. All FREE money for the taking.

Principle 4: Take Advantage of Other Tax-Advantaged Savings Accounts

We've discussed the retirement accounts that can be set up when employed by a company. However, not all companies offer them, or you may want to invest more than the company 401(k) allows. Well, there's some good news. Depending on the country and the purpose of the account, other tax-advantaged options exist.

IRA's, SEP-IRA's, ROTH-IRA's – United States

If you are not in a company **401(k),** you can make some contributions up to a specific limit. The limit may change every year, so check to ensure you know the maximums. If you're 50 years of age or older, there's an additional contribution you can make. It's called the Individual Retirement Account (IRA). This account gives you an immediate tax deduction, and the investment grows tax-free. The withdrawals are taxed as income at retirement, but you will likely be in a lower income tax bracket at that time.

So, what if you don't work for an employer? What if you own your own business? Well, if you operate your own business, you can start a **SEP (Simplified Employee Pension) –IRA**. You can contribute up to 25% of your self-employment income to a specific identified limit or a prescribed dollar value that fluctuates every year. You will need to confirm what the amount on an annual basis.

Finally, there is the **Roth-IRA**. This is another individual retirement account. This account doesn't extend an immediate tax deduction; money contributed is on an after-tax basis. However, the investment gains AND the withdrawals are NOT taxed.

RRSPs and TFSAs – Canada

Canada offers similar tax-advantaged schemes, but with a few differences from the American ones. The **RRSP (Registered Retirement Savings Plan)** is an investment vehicle for employees and the self-employed. One can use pre-tax money (through the employer), or after-tax funds from their own earnings to fund the account. This is in addition to a DC plan that an employee may participate in but is governed by limits. The plan offers a tax deduction, and the investment grows tax-exempt until withdrawals are made at retirement.

The **TFSA (Tax-Free Savings Account)** is an account available in Canada that provides tax benefits for savings. One uses after-tax earnings, and there is no immediate tax deduction. However, any income, including capital gains and dividends earned in a TFSA, is not taxed. Withdrawals can be made at any time (don't have to wait until retirement), and there are contribution limits. This account can be used for short to medium savings like saving up for down payment, vacation, car, etc.

Principle 5: Don't Make Withdrawals before You Retire

The whole point of putting money away for retirement is … that you use it for retirement. Don't treat it like funds to be used in an emergency. That's what emergency funds are for, and we reviewed the importance of setting one up in the "**PLAN**" section of the book.

In some countries, the government allows you to make withdrawals under certain conditions. For instance, your DC plan is locked in until retirement. However, in Canada, withdrawals from a Registered Retirement Savings Plan (RRSP) are allowed for a couple of exceptions and under certain conditions.

The Two (2) Exceptions

1. To Buy Your First Home

You and your spouse each can borrow up to $25,000 from your RRSPs for a down payment on your **<u>first</u>** home under the Canadian government's Home Buyers' Plan (HBP). The intent of this program is to help individuals get into homeownership. You don't pay any tax on the money as long as you pay it back over the next 15 years.

2. To Pay for Your Education or Training

You and your spouse each can borrow up to $20,000 from your RRSPs to pay for full-time or part-time education or training expenses under the government's Lifelong Learning Plan (LLP). This program is intended to help individuals upgrade their education and skills to obtain better or additional employment opportunities. The maximum one can take out in any year is $10,000. You don't pay any tax on the money that is withdrawn as long as you pay it back over 10 years.

The Costs of an Early Withdrawal

If your situation doesn't fall under the above exceptions, you can still make a withdrawal, but there are some downsides. Specifically, there are three costs.

1. You'll have to pay tax on your RRSP withdrawals.

Remember, you received a tax break when you made the initial contribution. If you take any money from your RRSP, the government will charge a withholding tax. The amount you pay depends on your withdrawal amount and where you live in the country.

2. You'll permanently lose RRSP contribution room.

There are contribution limits to your RRSP. Once you take money out, you can't replace the amount you had previously put into your registered savings plan. This reduces the potential value of your RRSP when you're ready to retire.

3. You'll miss out on the advantages of compound interest.

You will recall that these retirement savings accounts work the best with long-term, regular contributions and returns. The magic of compounding is eroded when you take the money out of your RRSP early. You lose the opportunity to earn money while it's invested. This obviously defeats the whole purpose of starting early and making contributions through your working career.

Summary

As citizens, we are taxed by governments so they can provide infrastructure, social programs and education to name a few. Depending on which country you're from, the day that you actually start working for yourself, "Tax-Freedom" day varies widely. However, I'm sure we all believe that we're paying far too much of our hard-earned dollars to the government. Therefore, when the government gives us an opportunity to reduce taxes for investments we will use in the future, we should take advantage of this scheme.

Different countries have different incentives when it comes to tax-advantaged investments. However, there are some sound principles to follow:

- Start as young as possible and use the power of time and money to exponentially grow your investment.
- As much as possible, use pre-tax dollars so that more funds in your account have the potential to grow by the magic of compounding.
- Never, ever miss an employer match – why? Because it's FREE MONEY.

- If your country has additional tax-advantaged incentives, strongly consider these options as they further reduce your tax burden while providing more investment funds in the long term.
- Don't make early withdrawals of these investments as there may be fees and penalties associated with this action. More importantly, you are "dipping" into savings that were earmarked for future years, so you'd be defeating the purpose of why you invested in them in the first place.

Go All Out on Tax-Advantaged Investments: Action Steps

Now it's your turn. Go to the *Fast Track to Prosperity Workbook* and do the exercise that lists your tax-assisted investments like the one shown below.

This chart can be found at
www.fasttrack2prosperity.com/bonus
Or scan this QR code with your phone camera.

If you currently do not have any of these, consider starting to invest in a tax-assisted investment.

Retirement Accounts, Pension Plans and Other Tax-Assisted Investments				
Name of Account	**Current Value (as of DD-MM-20XX)**		**Year I Plan to Use (if known)**	
Company A Pension Plan	$50,000		2030	
Registered Retirement Account	$100,000		2028	
Tax-Free Savings Account (TFSA) Canada	$5,000		2025	
Total	**$155,000**			

1. Are you using pre-tax dollars? If possible, use pre-tax rather than after-tax dollars to fund these accounts.
2. If you work for an Employer, find out through company resources or Human Resources, whether there is a Company match for contributions you make to the Company retirement plan. If there is, are you taking advantage of this FREE MONEY?
3. Are there other Tax-advantaged Savings/Investment accounts in your country that you can participate in? Your country government's website or offices will be a good source of information on their availability.

17

NEVER HAVING TO SAY "NO" TO THE EXTRA GUACAMOLE

As we come to the last chapter of the book, I want to devote some time to how you can continue to PROSPER. We've reviewed several strategies for investing that will place you in a good position going forward. Still, I also want to propose some sound tips and techniques to better manage your finances, which can make a difference starting **TODAY**! I'll refer to these as "hacks." Don't worry,

I'm not going to ask you to give up your expensive, flavored coffees or those things in life that give you joy.

There are many books out there asserting that doing away with coffee will make you rich. Author David Bach coined the phrase "The Latte Factor," meaning that little expenses can really add up.[1] A $5 a day coffee can add up to $1,825 a year. Or the Australian real estate mogul who made the bold and ridiculous claim that millennials could never own a home because they spend too much money on avocado toast.[2] He no doubt received some heat for making such a preposterous statement. Just do the math! One would have to eat thousands of $20 avocado toasts to make up the cost of any real estate property.

Remember the Spending Margin in the PLAN portion of the book? If you manage your finances according to the PLAN, you can use your spending margin on anything that brings you joy. Even a triple, dark mocha, skinny, frozen almond milk latte, if that's what you want…or **never having to say "no" to that extra guacamole**.

In the Financial Literacy Program (FLP), we cover many practical money-ideas. It's interesting because as we're in the midst of brainstorming, many participants come up with even more ways to save money. The point is that once we get into the routine practice of cutting expenses and we taste victory, more opportunities to do the same will present themselves. As the adage goes: success breeds success.

Although we cover numerous money savings ideas in the FLP, I can only share a few here due to book-length restrictions. They will, however, get you started on improving your financial management. These ideas will teach how to:

- Stop overspending (we've covered some in Chapter 9, White Flag Moments like cancelling unused subscriptions; and Chapter 13 Credit Card Use… Friend or Foe?)

- Make minor changes to your spending that you will not even miss

Savings Hack #1: Treat Spending as Hours of Work

When purchasing an item, think about how long you would have to work to pay for it. For instance, if you're thinking of buying a pair of new shoes for $50 and you earn $25 per hour, it would take you two hours of work to buy them. If you pay 20% in taxes, it's 2.5 hours for that lovely footwear.

Obviously, this is not something that you have to constantly calculate every time you spend money. Still, it is a great technique, especially for big-ticket items, or some of those frivolous items that pass our eyes.

Bonus for Kids: This is great for teaching kids the value of money, whether one uses mom or dad's hourly rate, or even better if they're working, their own to prove the point.

I know this simple idea has saved me lots of money over the years.

Savings Hack #2: Spend Free Month

You may have heard of challenges, whether for practical or religious purposes, where an individual gives up something for a period of time. With "Dry January", people voluntarily stop drinking alcohol after the excesses of December and start the New Year clear of alcohol. Lent is a time of fasting and abstinence in the Catholic Church. In both examples, people give up or forego something they usually enjoy partaking in.

Let's apply that to spending. How about a Spend free month? This is where you would give up any spending above your fixed expenses (housing, food, utilities, etc.) for a period of time. The advantages of this practice are that it brings your finances to a zero base, and you truly get an idea of your expenses and spending habits.

If a month seems too long, begin with two weeks and then next time, extend it to a month. When I recommend doing one of these for my clients, I also remind them not to overspend the month before and to have enough purchases made, so the spend-free month goes smoothly. That would defeat the whole purpose. No need to be dishonest with yourself.

I've used this similar technique specifically for groceries. I bought only perishables like milk, eggs and some vegetables for a month. I used this time to clean out my pantries and freezer of all the food that had been stored there from past purchases.

Savings Hack #3: Groceries

Behind our tax bill and housing costs, groceries or food is usually one of our largest expenses. And although food is not optional, how we spend on it is. It makes good sense to pay close attention to this cost. Even a 10-15% savings over the years for a family can translate into thousands of dollars in their pocket. This is certainly more desirable than the supermarkets benefiting from your hard-earned money. Here are some ideas to help manage the cost of groceries:

- Plan meals and then shop for groceries once a week, if possible. Sometimes the more you go to the market, the more you are likely to spend.
- *Never* shop when hungry. When famished, everything looks delicious, and you'll be more tempted to buy items you don't necessarily need.
- Use a list… and try to stick to it. This is simply effective planning, and then holding to the plan.
- Make use of rebates and frequent shopper programs. Many stores now offer these programs, often free of charge. If you're going to shop there,

you might as well take advantage of what they are offering.

- Choose a warehouse or superstore for bulk buying …but BEWARE of over-spending!!! These mega-stores are "popping up" everywhere in many urban centers. Ask yourself, are you really going to use that 24-pack of toothpaste?
- Companies spend millions of dollars every year on marketing campaigns that convince us to buy their products. Compare prices on store brands, name brands and no-name brands. Look at the ingredients list. Often, prices on these brands can be 20-50% lower than brand names ones with the same ingredients. In fact, the products often come from the same processing facility, just with another label. In other words, you may just be paying extra simply for the name-brand on the label.
- Learn to be a label reader and watch the scanner at the cash register for errors. Guess what? Technology is only as good as the people that program the systems. People make mistakes. In some countries, if the scanned price is different than the price marked on the shelf, the customer is entitled to the product for FREE or a further discount of the price.[3] This is called the "Scanner Price Accuracy Code of Practice," in Canada.
- Shop the clearance section or "Quick Sale" items, especially if you freeze the food item.
- Buy food on sale or in season. Depending on where you live, prices for imported fruit and vegetables can vary depending on the time of year. Can the family do without that "out-of-season" fruit for a few months to save some money?
- When there's a sale, stock up. Sale items can be a great deal, and most frequently used consumables

always go on sale. Toilet paper, dish soap, toiletries, etc. Being Italian, my dad would always buy olive oil and canned tomatoes by the case. If it's an item you frequently use, buy a bunch of them.

- Go to any major supermarket, and the layout is basically the same. Marketers have spent years studying our buying habits and know exactly how to design a store. You know those items we usually need on a weekly basis like milk, eggs and bread? Where are they located? Usually on the opposite end or close to the end of your shopping trip. Why? Because they want us to walk throughout the whole store and pick up many other products before getting to those staples we often need.
- The placement of articles throughout the store is strategic. You know all those items at the check-out counter? They are placed there because we tend to wait in line to pay for our groceries, and we have a tendency to pick things up and just add them to the cart. Be strong…Don't give in.

Bonus for Kids: I've always maintained that one of the greatest skills you can impart to young teenagers is how to grocery shop. Take them around a store and teach them how to read labels, prices, and other valuable tips. Imagine how much money they can save over their lifetime by mastering this one financial skill.

Savings Hack #4: Review your Insurance Policies and Increase your Deductibles

When buying insurance to cover your home, car or health, opt for the highest deductibles you can manage. The deductible is the portion you have to pay when making a claim. You pay the first part, and the insurance company pays the balance.

For instance, let's say you get into an accident with your car, and it costs $2,000 to repair and your insurance policy has a $500 deductible. You pay the first $500, and the insurance company covers the remaining $1,500.

Typically, the higher the deductible you choose, the lower the premium because you're taking on more of the risk should you make a claim. Obviously, you don't want to make any claims as this can increase your annual premiums, but LIFE happens, so you need to be prepared.

It's good to review your insurance policies every year and determine whether you need to make some changes. According to a survey by Value Penguin, a personal finance website, 47% of homeowners in the U.S. do not know what their homeowner insurance policies covers. In addition, nearly 20% have never reviewed their policies.[4] I know it contains a lot of legal terms, but you need to know what your insurance policy covers, and just as important, what it does not.

Do you have enough insurance to cover a loss, or are you over-insured in some areas? In both of these scenarios, you're either putting yourself at risk because you don't have enough insurance or paying too much. If that vehicle is getting older and you carry a low deductible, it may be time to increase that amount.

Always make these insurance decisions in conjunction with your overall financial situation. For example, if you're going to increase your deductible to $1,000, ensure you have at least that amount in your emergency fund should you need to draw on it. You don't want to make what you think is a good decision on your insurance and then go into debt to pay the deductible, should you have a claim.

Savings Hack #5: Pass on the Extended Warranties

You've been dreaming of having movie nights with a nice big-screen T.V. in your living room. The family is all around eating popcorn as you enjoy one of the latest movie releases. You go to the store, and after looking at some options, you finally pick out that T.V (and popcorn- maker) and go to pay for your purchases. Then, before finalizing the sale, the salesperson asks you that all-important question. "Do you want the extended warranty on those?" You think about it for a while, and a bit of fear crosses your mind. What happens if you're watching the latest series with the family and suddenly you get a black screen on that T.V? Or the popcorn machine, heaven forbid, stops popping? So, you make a quick decision and say 'yes' to the extended warranty.

First of all, a warranty protects the consumer if the product breaks and needs to be fixed or replaced. Warranties used to be offered predominantly on big-ticket items. Now, they are sold on almost everything, even small appliances like popcorn makers.

So, what's the issue with extended warranties?

- Conveniently, the sales person fails to tell you that these products already come with a manufacturer's warranty, so an extended warranty from the store or third party is not required. Remember the over-insuring discussion above?
- Selling extended warranties are another stream of income retailers rely on to generate revenue.
- Salespeople are paid handsomely (bonuses, extra compensation, time-off, etc.) for selling this additional coverage.
- The probability that the product will fail in the first five years is pretty low. Additionally, in five years, you may want to replace it rather than fix it, especially with electronic products. Think about how outdated a five-year-old cellphone or laptop is nowadays.

- Some extended warranties cost so much that you could have easily bought a new product with what you spent.

Specifically with cars, use the same general rule. The car manufacturer warranty is usually appropriate for the type of vehicle you are purchasing. The extended warranty offered by the dealership is just another stream of income for them. The mark-up profit on these additional warranties is very high, so don't get pressured to buy something you will likely never need.

Summary

In this chapter, we've looked at some ways to save extra money, so that there's more at the end of the month to use….. well, for whatever you choose. It's up to you! Get into the habit of looking for cost-saving ideas. That way, you never have to worry about saying "no" to the extra guacamole.

Never Having to Say "No" to the Extra Guacamole Action Steps

1. In Chapter 10, we learned about the Spending Margin. If you're implementing this plan for your finances, take time every few months to review your spending by category and see if there's ways to reduce, cut or save money. Even "fixed expenses" can be reduced by looking at the plan you're enrolled in (utilities) or the insurance policies (home, auto, life, etc.) that you may have.
2. Get the whole family involved in looking for those "savings hacks;" you'd be surprised at what ideas may come up that you hadn't thought of.

3. Consider the five "savings hacks" we reviewed in this chapter and incorporate them into your weekly, monthly, or annual spending.
4. Finally, celebrate and enjoy your successes of sound financial management.

Financial Literacy Program, Level 1, November 2019

Financial Literacy Program, Level 2, November 2019

Financial Literacy Program, Level 2, November 2019

CONCLUSION: PROSPERITY IN YOUR LIFE...IS JUST AHEAD!

As Barry Manilow sang, "Looks Like We Made It." Here we are, at the end. I applaud you for finishing the book. There's always something powerful and satisfying about completing a task, a project or even a reading like this and then checking it off as "completed." I've tried to highlight to you that we all make financial mistakes. Like a rodeo cowboy who falls off his horse, brushes himself off and jumps back on for the ride of his life. You can overcome any poor financial decisions and find prosperity.

If I've been successful, the end of this book is just the beginning of your journey to a prosperous life. It brings me great joy knowing that you've read this because you want to make a change in your financial life. I've done my best to cover a broad spectrum of personal finance topics that are key to prosperity. Simply, they are based on my life experiences.

The basic PAUSE, PLAN, and PROSPER model will help you on your financial journey. Whether you're just starting off, starting over, or a seasoned pro picking up a few tips, I trust you will find it of benefit to you. The decision on where you go from here is now yours.

As we near the end of this portion of your path to greater

financial literacy, I do want to leave you with a few departing thoughts:

- **Don't feel overwhelmed.** We covered a lot of information in this book. Don't let it overwhelm you to the point where you don't take any action. Re-read the material, especially focusing on the PAUSE part. This section lays the foundation for a wealthy and prosperous mindset.
- **Write it down.** Nothing is more important than putting your financial goals into writing and reading them daily. Using your financial core values, develop S.I.T.A.M.A goals and then measure your results often. Remember in Chapter 6: Specific, Intentional, Timeframe, Achievable, Measurable, and Accountability
- **Always be teachable**. There may be a few things in a book this length you may not agree with or feel is not for you. That's perfectly fine. Don't let that be a "stumbling block" in taking action on the things you are aligned with.
- **Take action.** Take some action…however small or imperfect. I didn't (and still don't) do all the things suggested in this writing perfectly. Don't be surprised if you don't either. But, I try to be mindful of what needs to be done and improve in each area. Remember that even a small change every day will add up over time and make a substantial difference in your financial success.
- **Beware of bad habits.** Be on guard with falling back to bad habits. If you apply the concepts we've outlined in this book, you will have success. You will have worked hard to make those changes and experienced progress in the various financial areas of your life. It can be easy to fall back into old ways

again, like adding more debt or making poor investment choices. Don't fall into that trap and if you do, be mindful and financially mature enough to recognize it and move on.

- **Money shame has no place here.** I'd be amiss if I didn't reiterate the importance 'money shame' can play in your quest for financial wellness. Again, this is very real and imperative that you recognize it early and don't allow it to thwart your progress. Money shame can come at us from our families, friends or even external sources like social and news media. But, more often than not, we tend to bring it on to ourselves with constant negative self-talk and the refusal to move on from an adverse financial event.

Just as important, now that you understand this concept and its prevalence, be mindful and provide support to those that may be experiencing this emotional setback. Help could be anything from just "lending an ear" to helping them find professional assistance with their consent. You could be making a significant difference in their future.

- **Prosperity is more than just money.** As I outlined in my letter initially, being prosperous isn't just about money. It encompasses health, relationships, spirituality and much more. But now that you know how to fast track yourself to prosperity – you can define what it means to you. You have a blueprint to prosper financially. It's not just some mythical thing that happens to lottery winners and financial experts. And you can use your money to design your own prosperous life.
- **The power of financial education.** Financial literacy, awareness and success are powerful. It will

change your life for the better. Now that you have that knowledge and experience, the best thing you can do is share your experiences and learnings with others. Start at home, with your spouse, partner and most importantly, your children. Remember, they are likely not getting any financial training in the education system. Passing on your core values and learnings will be one of the best legacies you can provide them.

- **Pay it forward.** Finally, as you become prosperous and it changes your life, remember that you can also change the lives of others. Whether big or small, you can make a difference, whether financially or in other ways, to those who may not be as fortunate or could use the support.

As we end here, I want to wish you success and prosperity. I feel privileged to have shared a piece of my life with you. And I'm not really gone for good. I'd love to hear from you. If you have a question, need some encouragement or just some fine-tuning in your financial education, I'd be honored to help. Some of my students from my early day classes still contact me now and then with questions or to share their progress and achievements. It brings me great joy to know that I've helped them in their journey to prosperity.

I would love to hear from you. Please send me an e-mail (jay@fasttrack2prosperity.com) and tell me what you've learned from this book. It'd be great to continue our connection.

Lastly, as promised, there are several bonus resources throughout the book to help you with your financial education. You can get them at www.fasttrack2prosperity.com/bonus and the various calculators are at www.fasttrack2prosperity.com/calculators.

ACKNOWLEDGMENTS

When I was approached with the idea of writing a book, I thought it would be daunting task. Well, I wasn't disappointed! It's been one of the hardest projects I have undertaken but also one of the most rewarding. This book would not have been possible without the love, support and hard work of many people.

I would like to give special thanks to Rory Carruthers and his marketing team at Lasting Press publishers for guiding me through the whole book writing process. Additionally, to Christopher Bright, Crystal Davis, and Carly Carruthers, thank you for your insight, I learned so much from our weekly calls and support you've provided on my progress.

Thanks to Jody Sneddon for the numerous brainstorming chats and ideas on how to make this writing more relatable to a vast, general audience.

I am extremely grateful to my editor, Marlene Lane, the "Grammar Queen," whose keen eye made this the best it could be. And one of the best complements I could receive was that she actually learned something about personal finances through the editing process.

To my talented Illustrator, Dzianis Davydau, thank you designing caricatures that reflected the message I wanted to convey.

Laolu Tubi, thank you for making me look good. I appreciate the photoshoot and the nice pics for the book cover.

To my parents, thank you for being incredible role models and teaching me the importance of hard work, doing what is right and unconditional love.

Immense gratitude to my uncle Tony Falcone, who himself was a gifted educator, avid reader, and consummate storyteller. And although he was not here in person, his presence was felt throughout this entire book writing process. Only wishing you were here to see, read, and debate the final product.

To the Multicultural Association of Wood Buffalo (MCAWB) past and present staff. Anurag Martur and Therese Greenwood, thank you for allowing me to use your organization as a platform to reach the many newcomers to Canada and giving me the latitude to teach the material.

I would like to extend my deepest gratitude to the hundreds of past students of the Financial Literacy Program, thank you for the privilege of imparting my experiences to you. It has been a pleasure coming alongside of you, learning about your experiences and hopefully helping you on your financial journey. You have given me a renewed life purpose and I'm forever thankful for you.

Finally, to my new readers, thank you for picking up this book. I hope and trust it helps you *Fast Track to Prosperity*.

ABOUT THE AUTHOR

Jay Falcone, *B. Comm, MBA, CMA, CPA, CHRP* has devoted over 35 years in the Financial and Human Resources industry, including a decade in Pension and Benefits and several years as an educator. He has a passion for personal finance and has developed the Financial Literacy Program (FLP) for the Multicultural Association of Wood Buffalo in Fort McMurray, Alberta, Canada. Through his unique and fun teaching style, Jay has taught hundreds of newcomers to Canada basic and advanced financial concepts.

Jay is the founder of Prospero Financial Solutions Ltd., a company that provides financial education workshops and seminars to educational institutions and small to mid-size companies. He is a graduate of the University of Alberta and Royal Roads University.

Born and raised in Edmonton, Alberta, Jay moved to Fort McMurray to begin his career and where he has since called home. As a passionate and consummate foodie, you might even get a glimpse of him giving an Italian culinary lesson in the community or for a corporate cooking event.

ABOUT THE AUTHOR

TAX FREEDOM DAY REFERENCES

Australia – Centre for Independent Studies

- https://www.cis.org.au/commentary/opinion/tax-freedom-day-2019-is-april-17-extra-day-of-tax-burden-added-since-2018/

United States – Tax Foundation

- https://web.archive.org/web/20060423204907/http://www.taxfoundation.org/taxfreedomday/

New Zealand – Staples Rodway

- https://www.stuff.co.nz/business/money/92335535/tax-freedom-day-has-arrived-and-so-has-the-time-to-talk-about-tax-fairness

Uruguay – CPA Ferrer

- https://web.archive.org/web/20140218004721/http://www.cpa.com.uy/

South Africa – Free Market Foundation

- http://www.freemarketfoundation.com/

Brazil - Instituto Brasileiro de Planejamento Tributario

- http://www.ibpt.org.br/

Italy – CGIA

- https://quifinanza.it/fisco-tasse/tasse-un-2-giugno-che-somiglia-al-25-aprile-giorno-di-liberazione-fiscale/170895/

United Kingdom – Adam Smith Institute

- https://en.wikipedia.org/wiki/Tax_Freedom_Day#cite_note-6

Canada – Fraser Institute

- https://www.fraserinstitute.org/article/june-14-is-tax-freedom-day-in-canada-but-dont-pop-the-champagne-yet

Spain – Foundation for the Advancement of Liberty and Spanish Taxpayer's Union

- https://en.wikipedia.org/wiki/Tax_Freedom_Day#cite_note-5

Germany – Bund der Steuerzahler

- https://web.archive.org/web/20160625222912/http://www.steuerzahler.de/Von-1-Euro-bleiben-nur-476-Cent/65996c76569i1p1520/index.html

Israel – Jerusalem Institute for Market Studies

- https://web.archive.org/web/20130913073944/http://www.jims-israel.org/TFD2013.aspx

France - Institut Economique Molinari (IEM)

- http://www.institutmolinari.org/la-pression-sociale-et-fiscale,3426.html

Belgium - Institut Economique Molinari (IEM)

- http://www.institutmolinari.org/la-pression-sociale-et-fiscale,3426.html

RESOURCES

Note: The following calculations are based on estimates using the calculators. Results are approximations.

Loan Calculator – Debt-Repayment

To calculate how much you need to put towards your debt to pay it off in a specific amount of time, use the Loan Calculator – Debt Repayment at www.fasttrack2prosperity.com/calculators.

Example: You have an $8,000 bank loan for some renovations you just finished. The loan has a 4.8% interest rate with a minimum payment of $100 to be paid off over 5 years.

Determine the monthly payment required to pay off this debt in 5 years. In the calculator, enter the following:

Choose the calculation	Find the monthly payment
Loan amount	$8,000
Interest rate	4.8%
Number of months	60 (5 yrs. X 12 months)
Calculate	
Monthly Payment	Answer: $150.24

The calculator gives you a monthly payment of $150.24. We will use $150 for our purposes. Therefore, in addition to the $100 minimum payment, an additional $50 ($150-$50) will be required to pay down this $8,000 loan in 60 months. The extra $50 is considered Important Savings.

Loan Calculator – Debt-Payoff Calculator

To determine how long it will take you to pay off a loan, debt or liability at your current interest rate, use the Loan Calculator – Debt Payoff at www.fasttrack2prosperity.com/calculators .

Example: You have a Line of Credit loan of $10,000 at 4.5% with a $200 monthly payment.

Choose the calculation	Find the number of months
Loan amount	$10,000
Interest rate	4.5%
Monthly payment	$200
Calculate	
Number of months	Answer: 55

It would take you 55 months to pay down this loan at the current rate of $200 per month.

Mortgage Calculator

To calculate how much the monthly mortgage payment would be for a certain mortgage amount, use the Mortgage Calculator at www.fasttrack2prosperity.com/calculators.

Example: You have a $400,000 mortgage at 3.0% and an 18-year amortization period.

Determine the monthly mortgage payment by entering the following in the calculator:

Choose the calculation	Find the monthly payment
Mortgage amount	$400,000
Mortgage term	18 years
Interest rate	3.0 %
Calculate	
Monthly Payment	Answer: $2,398.89

The calculator gives a monthly mortgage amount of $2,398.89 or about $2,400. Let's say, that you've managed your finances well and have a financial goal of eliminating your mortgages in 13 years instead of 18. To determine how much of an extra monthly payment, you would have to make, change the mortgage term number to 13 and you'll get a monthly payment of $3,099.68 or $3,100. Therefore, if your current monthly payment is $2,400, the additional amount required is $700 per month ($3,100 - $2,400). However, discuss this plan with your bank to ensure your mortgage allows extra payments.

Savings Goal Calculator

There will be times when you have a goal to save a specific amount of money. To find out how much you have to save every year, use the Savings Goal calculator at www.fasttrack2prosperity.com/calculators. The Savings Goal is how much you'd like to save; the Saving Period is how long in years you will be saving for your goal. Finally, Making Deposits is how often you will be contributing to your goal and the Interest Rate, is how much your savings will generate while achieving your goal.

Example: Let's say you have a goal to save $30,000 over the next 7 years to buy a property. The investment return from your savings account will be 3.0 % and you want to calculate the monthly deposit required.

Choose the calculation	Find the monthly deposit required to meet your Savings goal
Savings Goal	$30,000
Savings Term	7 years
Making Deposit	Monthly
Interest rate	3.0 %
Calculate	
Monthly Deposit	Answer: $320.55

To reach your savings goal, you would need to deposit $320.55 per month or ($3,846.60 annually $320.55 X 12 months) for the next 84 months (7 years).

Investment Inflation Calculator

To find out how much your savings will grow to over a long period of time, you can use the Investment Inflation

Calculator at: www.fasttrack2prosperity.com/calculators. This tool is especially beneficial for calculating retirement savings.

Example: You have a gross annual salary of $60,000 and have a goal to save 10% per year ($6,000) for your retirement. This translates to a monthly contribution of $500 per month. If you plan to retire in 30 years and estimate the rate of inflation to be 3% per year, while earning 6% on the investment, how much will your account be worth after this period of time? You have $0 as a starting balance.

Choose the calculation	The Return on Investment
Investment amount (starting balance)	$0
Number of years	30 years
Interest rate	6.0%
Compounding	Monthly
Contributions	$500
Frequency	Monthly
Annual Inflation rate	3.0%
Calculate	
Future Value	Answer: $502,257.52

The amount your investment will grow to in 30 years is $502,257.52.

NOTES

1. The Financial Landscape

1. Lu, Marcus (2021, May). Visualizing the Snowball of Government Debt. *Visual Capitalist.* https://www.visualcapitalist.com/government-debt-in-2021
2. Ali, Aran (2021 May). The state of Household debt in America. *Visual Capitalist.* https://www.visualcapitalist.com/the-state-of-household-debt-in-america
3. By Staff – The Canadian Press (2021 June). Canadian consumers are now carrying $2.1 T ($1.47 USD) in debt, driven by mortgages. *Global News.* Canadian consumers are now carrying $2.1 trillion in debt, driven by mortgages - National | Globalnews.ca
4. Pattie-Lovett Reid (2021 April). 53% of Canadians on the brink of insolvency: MNP survey. *BNN Bloomberg.* https://www.bnnbloomberg.ca/53% of Canadians on the brink of insolvency: MNP survey
5. (July 2018) Canadian and U.S. Residential mortgage arrears and foreclosure rates, *CMHC* https://www.bing.com/Canadian and U.S. Residential mortgage arrears and foreclosure rates CMHC
6. Adam McCann (May 2021) What is the average credit card interest rate?; *Wallethub,* https://wallethub.com/edu/cc/average-credit-card-interest-rate/50841
7. Joe Resendiz (March 2021) Average credit card debt in America: 2021, *Value Penguin by Lending Tree,* https://www.bing.com/Average+credit+card+debt+in+America+2021+Value+Penguin+by+Lending+Tree
8. 2017 Organization for Economic Co-operation and Development (OECD) Survey on G20/OECD Report on Adult Financial literacy in G20 p.8 http://t4.oecd.org/daf/fin/financial-education/G20-OECD-INFE-report-adult-financial-literacy-in-G20-countries.pdf
9. FP Canada, 2021 Financial Stress Index https://fpcanada.ca/planners/2021-financial-stress-index

3. What's Your Teachability Index (TI)?

1. Brown, Don (2014, July), What are the four most common causes of workplace injuries? *Safety Management Insights;*

https://info.basicsafe.us/safety-management/blog/what-are-the-4-most-common-causes-of-workplace-injuries
2. From Arrogance to Naivete - the Teachability Index, https://theemergencesite.com/Tech/FourStates-of-Learning-Wk061009.htm

4. Core Values - Let's Dig Deep

1. The Cashlorette 2017, Nearly Half of Americans in Serious Relationships Argue over Finances, viewed February 14, 2022, < https://www.prnewswire.com/news-releases/nearly-half-of-americans-in-serious-relationships-argue-over-finances-300499003.html>
2. MVOrganizing 2021, Why does financial problems cause divorce? Viewed February 14, 2022, <https://www.mvorganizing.org/why-does-financial-problems-cause-divorce/>

6. Goals with Holes

1. Hill, Napoleon (2007). *The Magic Ladder to Success*. Jeremy P. Tarcher. p.73-74
2. Wissman, Barret. (2018, March) An Accountability Partner Makes You Vastly More Likely to Succeed. *Entrepreneur*. https://www.entrepreneur.com/article/310062
3. MacKenzie, Gray. (2022) If You Can't Measure It, You Can't Improve It | Lessons from Peter Drucker. GuavaBox, LLC. https://guavabox.com/if-you-cant-measure-it-you-cant-improve-it/
4. (2020) The Complete Guide to Getting Rich, Deep Dive into your finances with help from some "Sharks" p.66
5. Gardner, Sarah and Albee, Dave, "Study focuses on strategies for achieving goals, resolutions" (2015). Press Releases. 266

9. White Flag Moments

1. www.allainzlife.com/-/media/files/allianz/pdfs/newsroom/2018-allianz-generations-ahead-fact-sheet-3.pdf (allianzlife.com)
2. Debt due to Social Media? It's more common than you think. The Ascent, Lyle Daly, May 14, 2019

13. Credit Card Use...Friend or Foe?

1. Credit card statistics 2021: 65+ facts for Europe, UK, and US (spendesk.com) Experian
2. 23 Incredible Credit Card Statistics in Canada in 2021 (reviewlution.ca)

14. Careful: Handle Debt with Care

1. Do Americans Know How Much They Owe? The Atlantic, Gillian B. White. Americans Don't Know How Much Credit Card and Student-Loan Debt They Have - The Atlantic

15. The Path to Investing

1. The 100 Best Warren Buffett Quotes, Matthew Frankel, The Motley Fool, fool.com
2. Can a company live forever? Kim Gittleson, January, 19, 2012 BBC News, New York bbc.com

17. Never Having to Say "No" to the Extra Guacamole

1. The Latte Factor: 7 Key Lessons We Can Learn From A Cup of Coffee (forbes.com)
2. Millionaire tells millennials: if you want a house, stop buying avocado toast | Avocados | The Guardian
3. Scanner Price Accuracy Code - Retail Council of Canada
4. https://www.valluepenguin.com/Nearly Half of Homeowners Don't Know What Their Insurance Policy Covers - ValuePenguin

www.ingramcontent.com/pod-product-compliance
Lightning Source LLC
Chambersburg PA
CBHW031919190326
41519CB00007B/346

* 9 7 8 1 9 4 9 6 9 6 4 5 5 *